From the author of the Barefoot TEFL Teacher blog

Lesson Planning for Language Teachers

Evidence-based techniques for busy teachers

David Weller

Lesson Planning for Language Teachers

Copyright © 2019 by David Weller.

All rights reserved. No part of this book may be reproduced in any form or by any electronic or mechanical means including information storage and retrieval systems, without permission in writing from the publishers. The only exception is by a reviewer, who may quote short excerpts in a review.

Cover and illustrations designed by David Weller

Published by Stone Arrow Publishing
www.stonearrowhq.com

Visit the author's website at:
www.barefootTEFLteacher.com

Printed in the United Kingdom

First Printing: May 2019

First Edition

ISBN-9781099456428

To Jake, Ross, and all the other language teaching legends out there.

CONTENTS

1 Introduction — 1
  1.1 Welcome — 2
  1.2 Why Lesson Plan? — 4
  1.3 Lesson Planning Process — 7
  1.4 How to Use This Book — 9

2 Students — 11
  2.1 Who Are Your Students? — 13
  2.2 What If You Don't Know Your Students? — 15

3 Aims — 16
  3.1 What Are Aims? — 17
  3.2 What's in an Aim? — 19
  3.3 Aims & Coursebooks — 23
  3.4 How Do You Write an Aim? — 25
  3.5 Personal Aims — 28

4 Context — 29
  4.2 How to Set a Context — 31

- 4.3 Running a Context Through a Lesson — 34
- 4.4 Context vs. Coursebooks — 35
- 4.5 Four Kinds of Context — 37

5 Structure — 39
- 5.1 Lesson Methodologies — 41
- 5.2 Presentation, Practice, Production — 43
- 5.3 Engage, Study, Activate — 49
- 5.4 Test, Teach, Test — 53
- 5.5 Task-Based Language Teaching — 57

6 Activities, Exercises, Tasks & Materials — 63
- 6.1 Definitions — 64
- 6.2 Activities & Exercises — 65
- 6.3 More Activities — 69
- 6.4 Task Design — 73
- 6.5 Using Materials — 79

7 Supporting Students — 83
- 7.1 Interaction Patterns — 85
- 7.2 Personalising the Coursebook — 89
- 7.3 Scaffolding — 93
- 7.4 Differentiation — 96

8 Assessment — 100
- 8.1 Checking Understanding — 101
- 8.2 Checking Progress — 103
- 8.3 Self-Assessment — 107

9 Review — 108

- 9.1 What If I'm Too Busy to Plan? — 109
- 9.2 Lesson Planning Checklist — 111
- 9.3 Final Thoughts — 114
- 9.4 Resources — 115

References — 116
About the Author — 117

1. INTRODUCTION

1.1
Welcome

How long did you spend planning last week?

I'd guess either too long, or not enough. Too long because planning is hard to get 'just right', or not enough because your schedule is crazy right now.

I want to show you a framework that makes planning fast and effective. One that works for you and your students, for every lesson.

If you're short on time, it'll give you the best chance of delivering a good lesson.

If you want to go all out, I'll show you evidence-based techniques to plan *amazing* lessons.

Either way, you'll finish planning with time to spare, zero stress, and a great lesson for your students.

Let's get started.

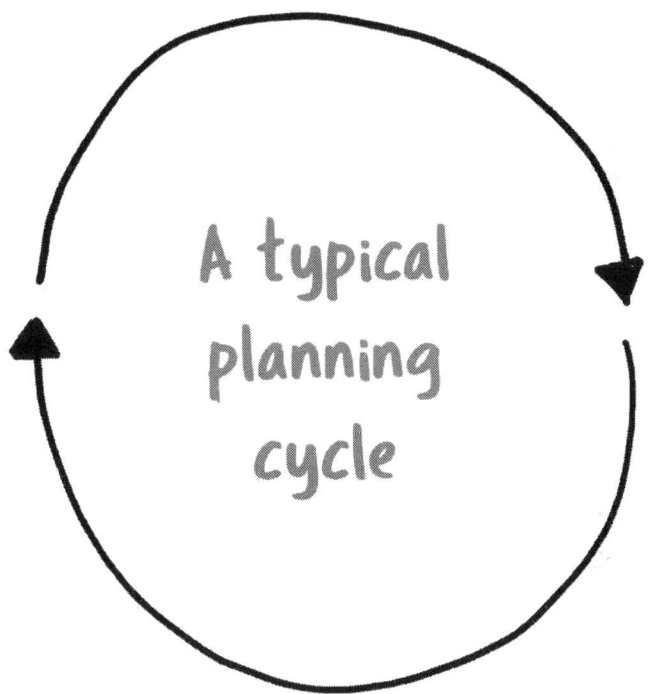

1.2
Why Lesson Plan?

There's a theory in the stock market that says everything known about a stock is reflected in its price.

It's the same with teaching. All your knowledge and current beliefs about teaching shine through in your plans.

By planning, you're giving each class the benefit of your unique experience, knowledge and style.

But lesson planning is hard, and it can take ages. It's easier to follow a coursebook, and students often expect it.

So why bother?

A plan helps you before class because it:

- Gives you a better chance of success
- Gives you confidence
- Reduces anxiety
- It's a reference in class, in case you forget what's next.

It can help you after class as well, as a reference to figure out what went well (and what not so well). Plus you can scribble notes on it for next time you teach that lesson.

Oh, and if you don't plan, your manager may fire you.

As most language teaching jobs require you to plan for every lesson, you'll be doing a lot of it. You might as well learn to do if faster, better, and

That's where I hope this book comes in.

I've collected my years of experience and combined it with the latest scientific data on what makes for effective teaching. I hope it'll give you a shortcut to improving your teaching.

Over the years I've seen lesson plans in every style, format and length. They are as individual as the teachers who make them.

I've seen great teachers walk into class with a post-it note, and not-so-great teachers using detailed ten-page plans.

The one thing I've noticed about all the great teachers I've met, is that they plan, reflect, and make small changes as a result.

If you combine that with the knowledge in this book, you'll see a huge improvement in your lesson planning, I promise.

Where are your students starting from?

↓

Where do you want them to get to?

↓

What's the best way for them to get there?

↓

How can you check their progress?

1.3
Lesson Planning Process

These four questions make up the fundamental planning process.

1. Where are your students starting from?

2. Where do you want them to get to?

3. What's the best way for them to get there?

4. How can you check their progress?

It's really the same planning process for anything, but applied to teaching.

You need to know where your students are at, linguistically. Then decide what you want them to achieve. Choose exercises, activities, tasks and materials that engage and support them. And decide what you'll need to see or hear that proves they're improving.

Simple? Yes.

Easy? Not exactly.

Let's look at each question in more detail.

Question	Section of Book
Where are your students starting from?	2. Students
Where do you want them to get to?	3. Aims
What's the best way for them to get there?	4. Context 5. Structure 6. Activities, Exercises, Tasks & Materials 7. Supporting Students
How can you check their progress?	8. Assessment

1.4
How to Use This Book

On the left you can see how each question relates to each section and chapter of this book.

Feel free to skip around and read whatever interests you. Although if you're new(ish) to lesson planning, I suggest reading all the way through once, to see how the concepts fit together.

If you're still with me, let's start with that first question; 'where are your students starting from?'

David Weller

2. STUDENTS

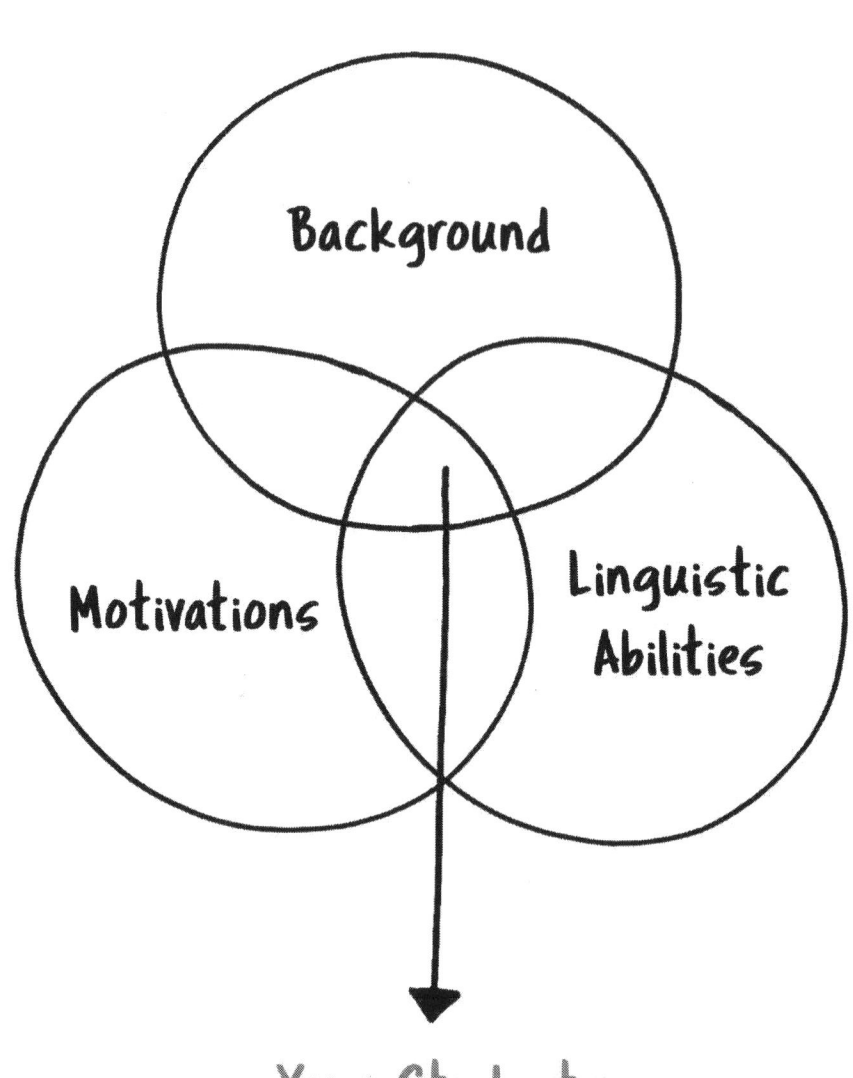

2.1
Who Are Your Students?

The better you know your students, the easier it is to plan. You'll also deliver better lessons, they'll learn more, and you'll all have more fun.

> *"The most important single factor influencing learning is what the learner already knows. Ascertain this and teach him accordingly."*
>
> *– David Ausubel (Ausubel 1968)*

Why?

Well, if you know their backgrounds (demographics), you can personalise topics to make your classes more engaging.

If you know reasons for learning English (psychographics), you can make the topics more relevant, which also increases engagement.

If you know their linguistic strengths and weaknesses, you can work on areas that are most useful for them.

Here are some questions for you to think about for each area.

Demographics

- Where are they from?
- What's their first language?

- How old are they?
- How long have they been studying?

Psychographics

- What are they interested in?
- What hobbies do they have?
- What else do they do in their free time?
- Who/what are the most popular celebrities, TV shows, music that most of them like?
- Why do they want to learn English? For tests, for travel, or because their parents are making them?

Linguistics

- What level are they?
- Do they have any fossilised errors (errors that they always make, even though they should know them?)
- Which areas of English do they struggle with? How about with grammar, and phonology?

The more of these you know, the better you're able to answer the first question in our lesson planning process – 'where are my students starting from?'.

2.2
What If I Don't Know My Students?

There are times when you won't know your students.

It could be the first lesson of a new class, or you're covering a class for a colleague.

It could be the way your school functions - students 'pay-as-they-go' and attend when they have time. Which means you don't know who'll be in any given class.

What do you do? Well, you do your best.

You'll need to plan with the information that you do know - their approximate language ability, age range, etc.

If you've been with the school a while, you may know regular students, or students you've taught in previous classes.

You can use items from the local news or events that you hear local friends talking about. If it's a talking point for them, it could be of interest to your students.

Students with the same learning background and demographic tend to make similar errors (especially noticeable with young learners). This is something you can consider when planning also.

3. AIMS

3.1

What Are Aims?

An aim is anything you want your students to achieve in a lesson.

Having an aim makes lessons more effective for learning (Hattie 2012). I like to choose two aims - one for my students and a personal aim for myself (see 'Personal Aims', p.28).

There are two ways of breaking down an aim; by the linguistic content (in the next chapter), and logistically (in the chapter 'How Do You Write an Aim?').

Yet for an embarrassingly long time, I didn't write aims. Yes, I learned all about them on my initial teacher training course. Yes, they made sense. But I was busy, and I'd been told to follow the coursebook ("two pages every lesson, and one page from the student's book for homework").

Surely my aims had just been set for me, for every lesson?

How little I knew.

While aims are often set by your school, syllabus or coursebook, you should relate those to what you know about your students.

Are they too easy, or too difficult? If so, can you adapt them? What would be best for the students to practice?

For the sake of spending one minute to set my aims, I could have improved much faster. Don't make the same mistake I did.

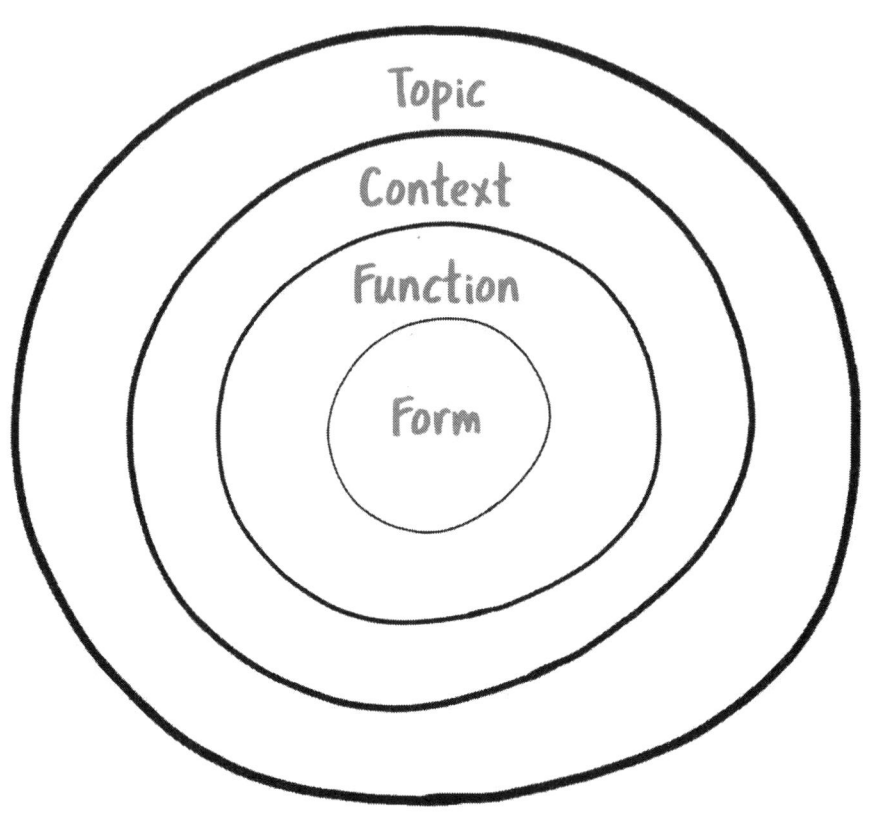

Four levels of language in lessons (and aims)

3.2
What's in an Aim?

A lesson aim should be a concise description of what you want to achieve by the end of the lesson.

It should also outline the topic, situation, and the language that's going to be used.

To do that we need to include four levels of language: a **topic**, a **context**, the **function** and the **form**.

These four levels I've adapted for classroom usage from the major levels of linguistics (Odell, Warriner, and Holt 2007).

These give your learners the essential 'what, where, why and how' of your lesson.

- **Topic** – the 'what' of the language. What's it about? Shopping, health, the Internet, ballet? Make it interesting for your learners. Bonus points if you find it interesting too!

- **Context** – the 'who, where and when' of the situation. Talking to a friend who's looking for a job? That's a context. Or booking a flight online for your next holiday? Also a context.

- **Function** – the 'why' of the language used. Why are they talking? Every time we communicate, it's for a reason. The function is that reason. Language doesn't exist independently of meaning.

- **Form** – this is what the language looks or sounds like. It's the phonology, lexis or grammar you're using. Are you using modal verbs for giving advice? A rising or falling tone for question tags?

Here's an example aim, with each level highlighted:

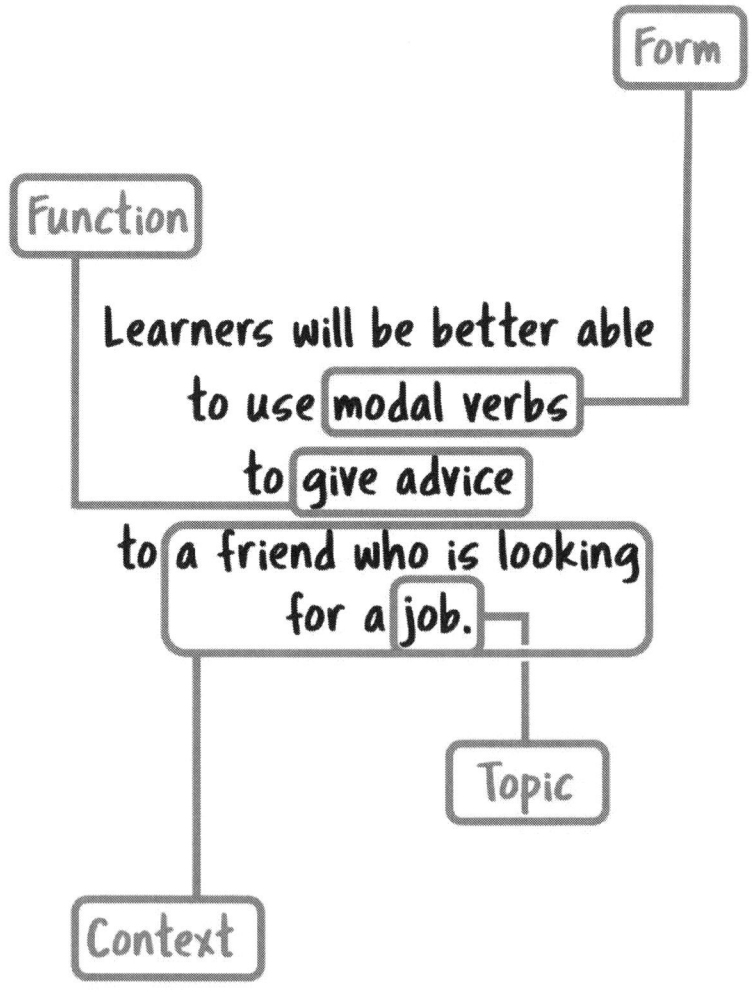

The last thing to remember (and perhaps the most important) is not to include too much new material in your aim.

We all want students to learn as much as they can, as fast as they can.

Studies on cognitive load theory show us that overwhelming the students with new information means that they don't retain most of it (Sweller 1988).

Keeping your aims modest (say, one main grammar or phonological point and/or a handful of new words) is enough.

David Weller

3.3
Aims & Coursebooks

To choose an aim, think of your students. What do they most need to know? It may not be what the course book says they should learn next.

Where possible, personalise the topic, context, function or form to better match your students' needs.

Saying that, don't get in trouble by not teaching what your school requires.

Use your common sense, and find a balance. If there's a real problem, then speak to your academic manager to see what can be worked out.

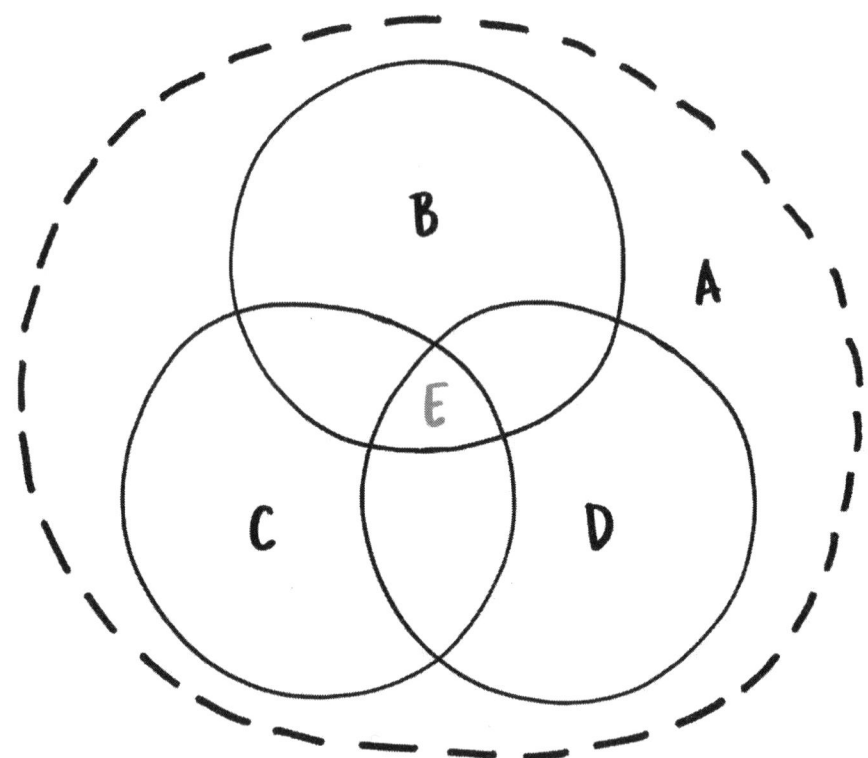

A: Required by syllabus
B: Learner-Centred
C: Specific
D: Observable
E: Good lesson aims!

3.4
How Do You Write an Aim?

We've already broken down aims by looking at linguistic content. Now we'll look at the logistics of writing an aim.

I always start my lesson plan aims with **'By the end of the lesson, learners will be better able to…'**

This gives every student the chance to achieve the lesson aim. If you write 'the learners will be able to…' then one of two things will happen:

- Every learner will achieve the goal (hurrah!) but that means it was too easy for most of the them (boo!)

- Weaker learners will be left behind, and not achieve the goal. Even the stronger learners may not be able to achieve it consistently.

I used to use the 'SMART' goal setting model (Specific, Measurable, Attainable, Relevant and Time-bound) (O'Neill 2000).

I don't anymore. As a concept designed for the business world, some aspects aren't best suited for teaching.

So instead I use the following criteria:

1. Required by syllabus/curriculum

Remember to stay within the rules of the curriculum that your school lays out. You don't want to get in trouble for ignoring the school rules.

2. Student-Centred

Think of your students! What topic and context will they find engaging? What level of language will be challenging but achievable?

3. Specific

Time to be specific. What exactly do you want them to learn? Remember the four levels of language? What is the function and form you will ask learners to focus on?

4. Observable

You're not a mind reader. Just because you teach it, doesn't mean that students learn it. Know what you're going to see, or hear, that tells you your learners are improving.

If you know this, you can use this to work backwards from, when planning the rest of your lesson.

Here's the same aim that we used before, but showing which parts of it are required, learner-centred, specific and observable:

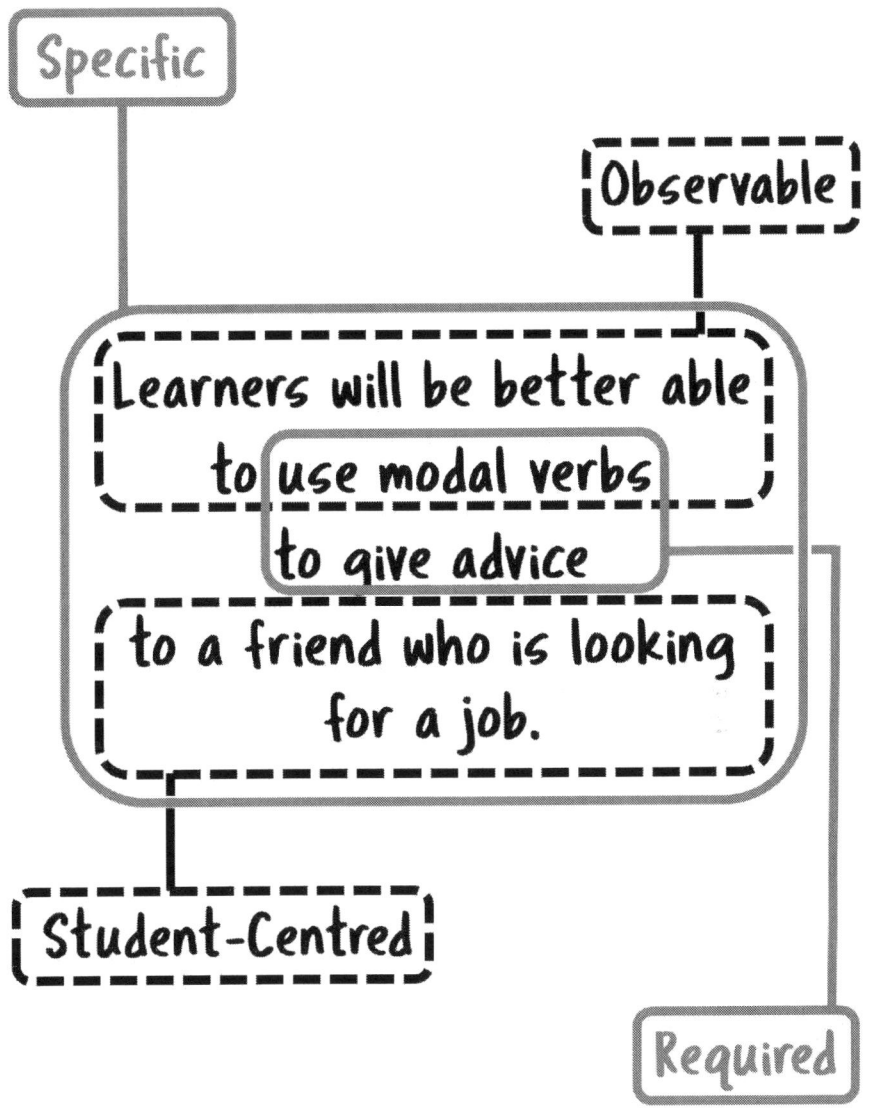

3.5
Personal Aims

A personal aim is something that you want to get better at by the end of the class.

This can be anything about your teaching that you want to improve.

If you're a newer teacher, this could be things like controlling the class, getting the timing right, or giving concise instructions.

More experienced teachers might look at differentiating to better help learners of different abilities, scaffolding, or trying out a different lesson structure.

Either way, having a personal aim helps to push yourself to develop as a teacher.

4. CONTEXT

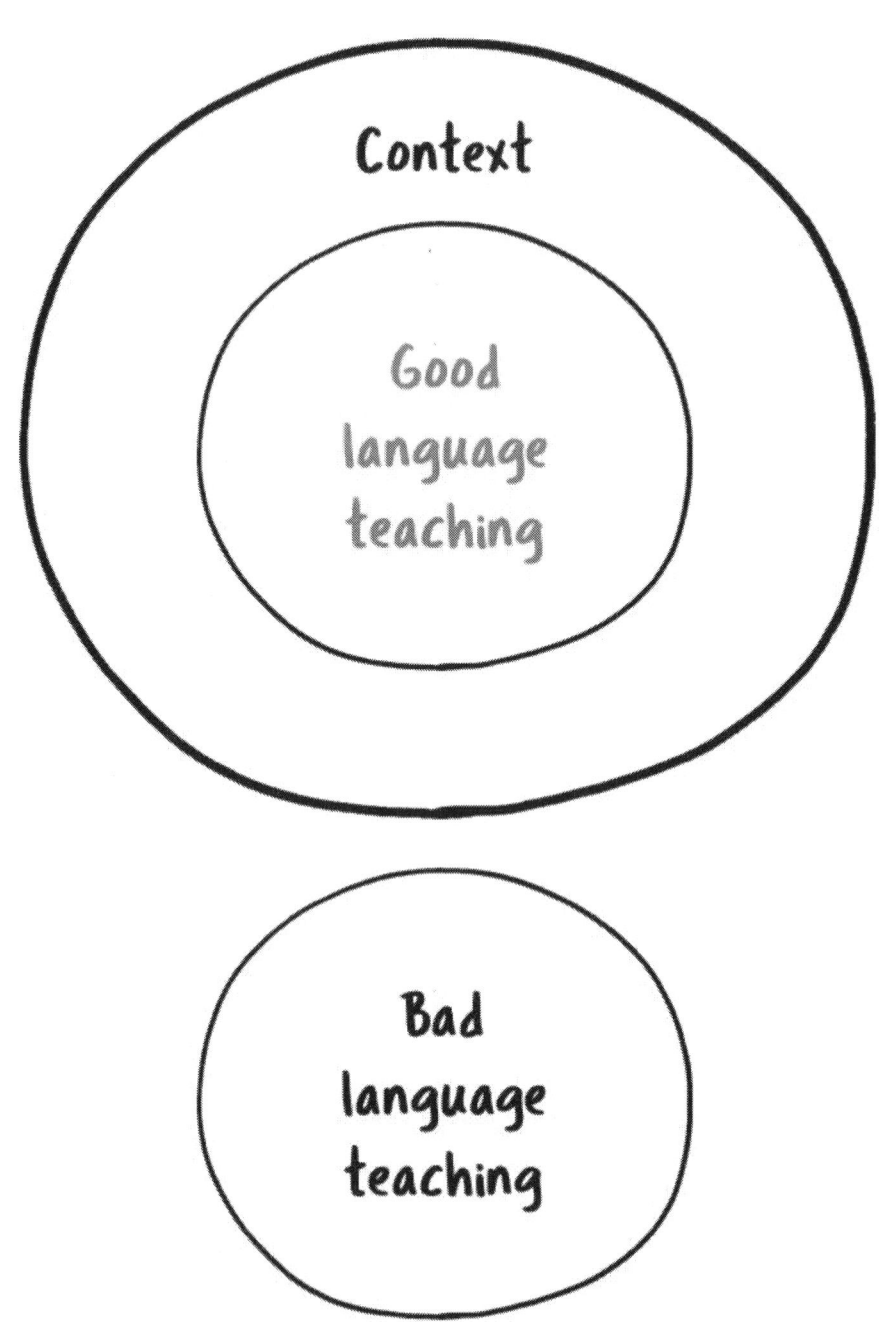

4.1
What is Context?

Every time we use language, it's in a context - a clearly set situation. The speakers know who they are, the relationship between them, where they are, and why the interaction is taking place.

If learners don't know the situation they're talking in, they'll find it harder to understand, use and remember the language. Students learn by repeatedly encountering language in context (Cook 2013).

Unfortunately, we often fall into the trap of getting learners to just practice the language – drilling or repeating sounds, words, patterns or dialogues – without them knowing why.

This can lead to confusion for our students. Why is it useful? Where can I use this without sounding like an idiot? Is it too formal/informal for some scenarios? How do I apply this outside the classroom?

Without context, we steal our learners' opportunity to have a meaningful interaction.

For example, at the start of class:

No Context

"Open your books and answer the questions on page 42"

Weak Context

"OK everyone, today we're going to talk about choosing a holiday. Tell your partner about your how you choose a holiday. Five minutes. Start."

Strong Context

"Hi everyone, great to see you all. Today's the last day before the holiday! Excited? I was, but my boyfriend and I argued last night about where to go on holiday…"

Hear the difference?

Even better is a context you know the learners are interested in (sports, local events, music, news, etc.), or will be useful (choosing a university, going to the doctors, booking a flight, etc.).

Context builds up connections that the learner is forming with the language, and shows them how language works in a realistic situation.

4.2
How to Set a Context

A context works best if it engages your students.

To make a context engaging, take a topic you know students will find interesting. Personalise it by asking for an opinion or asking them to share their experience with a partner.

Context setting can be set:

Verbally - tell the students a short anecdote and ask them what you should have done (opinion) or when something similar has happened to them (experience sharing)

Visually - show the students a photo, picture, or short video that grabs their interest. Ask them what they think is happening (opinion) or if they've ever been there / done that and what happened (experience sharing)

Aurally - play a song, an audio clip and ask what they think is going to happen (opinion) or what they could do (experience-sharing)

Using 'realia' – use real objects, bring in toys, photos, building bricks, magazines. Something that the learners can touch. Ask what they like most about it (opinion) or how it relates to them (experience sharing).

4.3
Running a Context Through the Lesson

Almost as important as setting a context is to run it throughout the lesson. Switching contexts can leave students confused.

Imagine – one minute they're using modal verbs to give advice to a friend looking for a job, the next they're giving advice to a colleague at work who's ill. Huh?

Sure, they're both using modal verbs, but stay in the same context unless you have a good reason to change.

If you want to make students aware of the other situations that they could use the language in, then do so at the end of the lesson (or recycle the language in another lesson, with a different context!)

This goes well with recycling materials, as this naturally keeps the context the same (see page 34).

4.4
Context vs. Coursebooks

Talking of coursebooks, I've not yet come across one that always matches your students.

As a teacher, you're normally required to follow a curriculum, which is delivered through a coursebook. A coursebook will normally suggest a topic, form and / or function for you. The better ones will choose a context for you as well.

Even if a context is included, at best it's disconnected from your learners, or at worst it bores them to tears. This is where your ingenuity and knowledge of your students comes in.

Ideally

- Choose a context that you know interests your learners
- Imagine yourself in that situation, having a conversation, and imagine the language you'd use
- Use that language in the class (perhaps modified to remove slang / profanity / or for a lower level)

Realistically

- Look at the coursebook to see which language you have to teach
- Imagine – when would you use it naturally?
- Think of a situation you could be in where you'd use it (and one that is engaging for the students)
- Use that situation and language in your class

Context Types

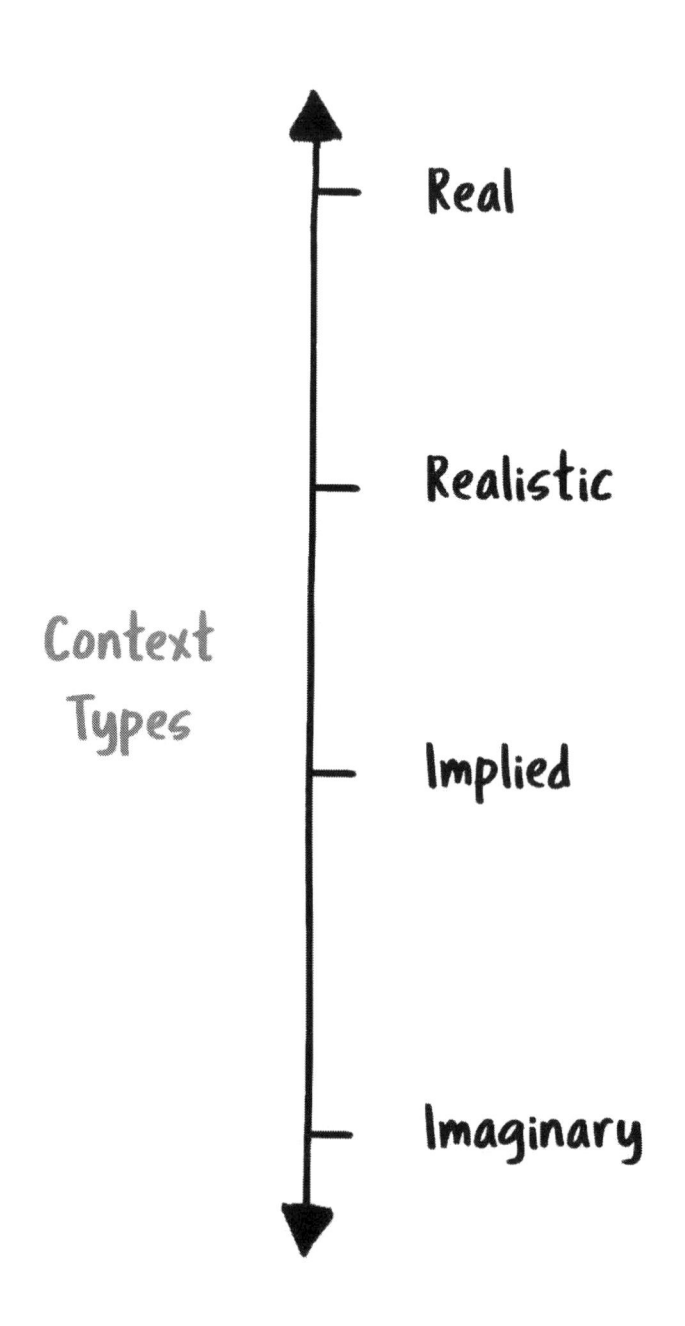

- Real
- Realistic
- Implied
- Imaginary

4.5
Four Kinds of Context

Don't fall into the trap of always choosing a realistic context.

Yes, it's easier to pick (you just think about a situation from real life), but it gets boring for you and your students.

I have a friend who describes this as the 'tyranny of context', and he's not wrong.

I would argue that there are four kinds of context. Imaginary, implied, realistic and real.

Real

Something that *actually* happens. When someone sets off the fire alarm. Or you spill coffee in your lap as you sit down. Or a student brings in a trophy they won yesterday. Something genuine, that can be discussed (If you don't have to exit the building in a hurry).

Realistic

Situations you might encounter in real life, but aren't happening right now. Visiting the doctor, going on holiday abroad, etc.

Implied

Regular topics or threads in your classes. Perhaps all your students watch the same TV series, and you can start talking about the characters.

Or it could be a running joke your class has, a regular activity you all do, or funny habits you have as a teacher – these can all be talked about.

Imaginary

Exactly that – imaginary situations. We do this with our friends all the time. It could be arguing who'd win in a superhero showdown. What you'd do if a zombie apocalypse happened tomorrow. Things you'd change as the leader of the country.

Think of it like this: when children play and create imaginary games, they all know precisely what they're doing. But if you pull a child aside and ask them to explain the rules, they can't. They just know.

Make your context as good as that. An absorbing situation that the students immerse themselves in. If everyone is clear *why* they're talking, it's a good context.

Use a mix of all these contexts, to keep your lessons fresh.

It also means you'll get to really know your learners, which helps with so many other things.

Remember to have fun!

5. STRUCTURE

Most lesson methodologies

1. Here's some stuff

2. Think about the stuff*

3. Use the stuff*

* Sometimes switched

5.1
Lesson Methodologies

Lesson methodologies (or lesson structures) are ways to sequence your lesson.

From your aims, you know what you want students to achieve. You know the language that you want to hear or see them produce by the end of the lesson.

You can use this as an end point in your planning. Choose a task that students can do at the end of the lesson which demonstrates this language.

Lesson structures are how we get to that final task.

At their core, all structures help us do the same things - introduce the language, think about the language, and use the language (as the diagram on the previous page flippantly shows). What changes is the order that they do these in.

In the last couple of decades, academics have moved away from the idea of set methods and structures in favour of teaching by principles (Richards and Renandya 2013).

However, for teachers (especially newer teachers), structures provide a starting framework that is useful and highly adaptable, as we'll see.

If you know the theory behind each structure, then you'll be able to adapt it to suit your students and your lessons.

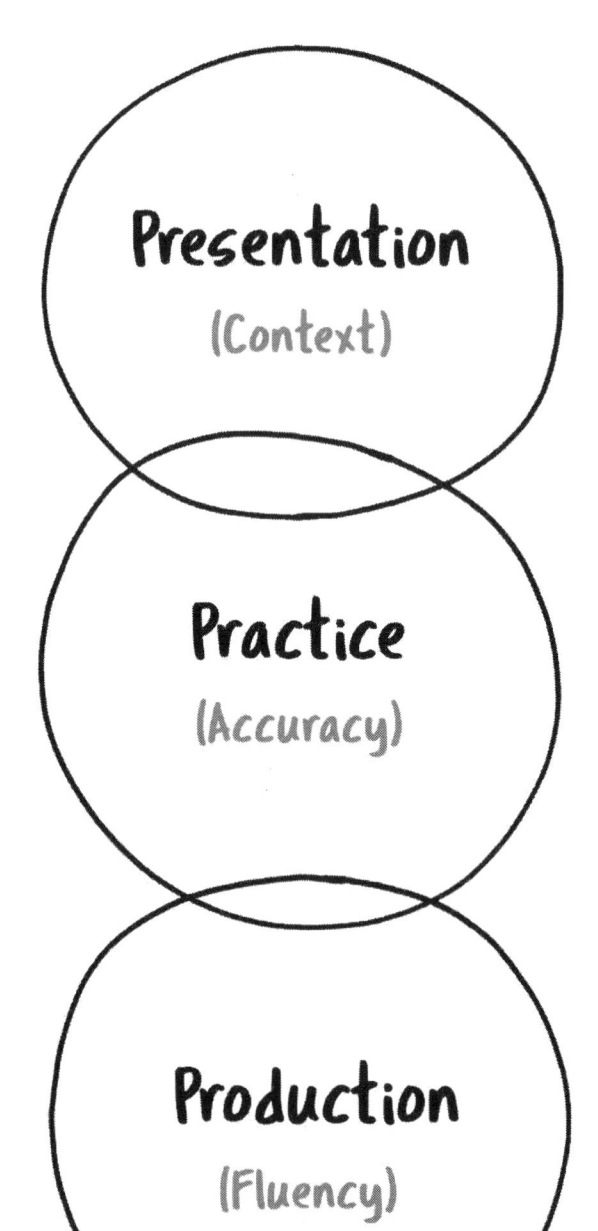

Presentation
(Context)

Practice
(Accuracy)

Production
(Fluency)

5.2
Presentation, Practice, Production

Old and getting a lot of criticism over the years, PPP is probably the most commonly taught structure on initial teacher training courses. It consists of three stages:

Stage 1: Presentation

This is where the language is introduced, or 'presented' to students in context.

This also helps them start to remember the language and vocabulary they already know about the topic.

The aim is to make sure students understand the context.

Stage 2: Practice

The 'practice' stage is when students use the language in a controlled way. This stage is sometimes divided into two - a controlled practice and a freer practice. You could get students to:

- Drill sentences or sounds, chorally or individually
- Do substitution drill in pairs
- Sentence match activities
- Gap fill exercises
- Pair work asking and answering questions

Error correction is important in this stage, so make sure you monitor the students closely. You could correct immediately, after the activity, or setup a peer-correction structure.

The aim of this stage is accuracy.

Stage 3: Production

This stage is where the language is used in a more open way. Things like role-plays, communication and collaborative tasks, discussion activities and debates.

The focus of this stage is using the language as fluently as possible.

Theory Behind PPP

This is where PPP gets criticised. It's an old structure, started in the 1960s, and language learning theory has developed a lot since then. Academics who study second language acquisition get annoyed that PPP doesn't tick any of the boxes for how we're supposed to learn a language (Lewis, 1996: 11)

Some learning assumptions behind PPP are:

- Students should be told the grammar rules, and then practice them (a deductive approach)
- Language learning is a skill like any other, and should be practiced as such
- Teacher control should be slowly handed over to students as the lesson progresses.
- Language is a series of items that can be learned in sequence
- The target language should be practiced by removing unnecessary language to help focus

All of these have been shown that this isn't how we best learn languages (in fact, the opposite is largely true!).

However, it isn't all bad. Here's my opinion on what the advantages and disadvantages are of PPP:

Advantages

- It's easy to learn for new teachers
- It's very flexible
- It's easy to plan for, and has a logical progression
- It works for most types of class, including larger classes
- Most course books use this, or a similar, method to structure their lessons and chapters

Disadvantages

- Research shows that it may not be the best way to teach or learn a language.
- Weaker students may overuse the target language from the practice session, sounding unnatural
- Students may not be sure how to use target language in different contexts
- Can be boring if used repeatedly for higher level students

Thoughts on PPP

Academics are often far removed from the classroom and the real world, and study phenomenon in isolation. Teaching over a period of time with PPP, you do see students improve.

Also, it's not done in isolation - you should be getting your students to interact in English and read extensively outside of class, for starters.

Presentation, Practice, Production works. Maybe not as well as something like TBLT (Task Based Language Teaching) but TBLT takes longer to plan and implement, which is difficult when your teaching hours are high.

Sure, it might not be theoretically perfect, but it does work.

Also, I believe it has evolved from the 'traditional' PPP. Here are some ways you can adapt the classic PPP structure:

- Spend more time eliciting in the presentation stage

- Turn the deductive aspect of explicit grammar instruction into an inductive aspect (i.e. students need to figure out grammar patterns themselves)

- Add collaborative tasks during the practice stage, where learners must use the target language to succeed

- Include more incidental language throughout the class, so learners hear language in a more natural context

- Change the final stage into a task, such as you'd find in 'Task-Based Language Teaching' (p.57)

These changes turn PPP into something else, a blended approach that addresses many of its criticisms.

The simplicity of PPP, combined with its renown, have kept it as probably the most widely used methodology. I doubt it's going away any time soon.

Engage
(Context)

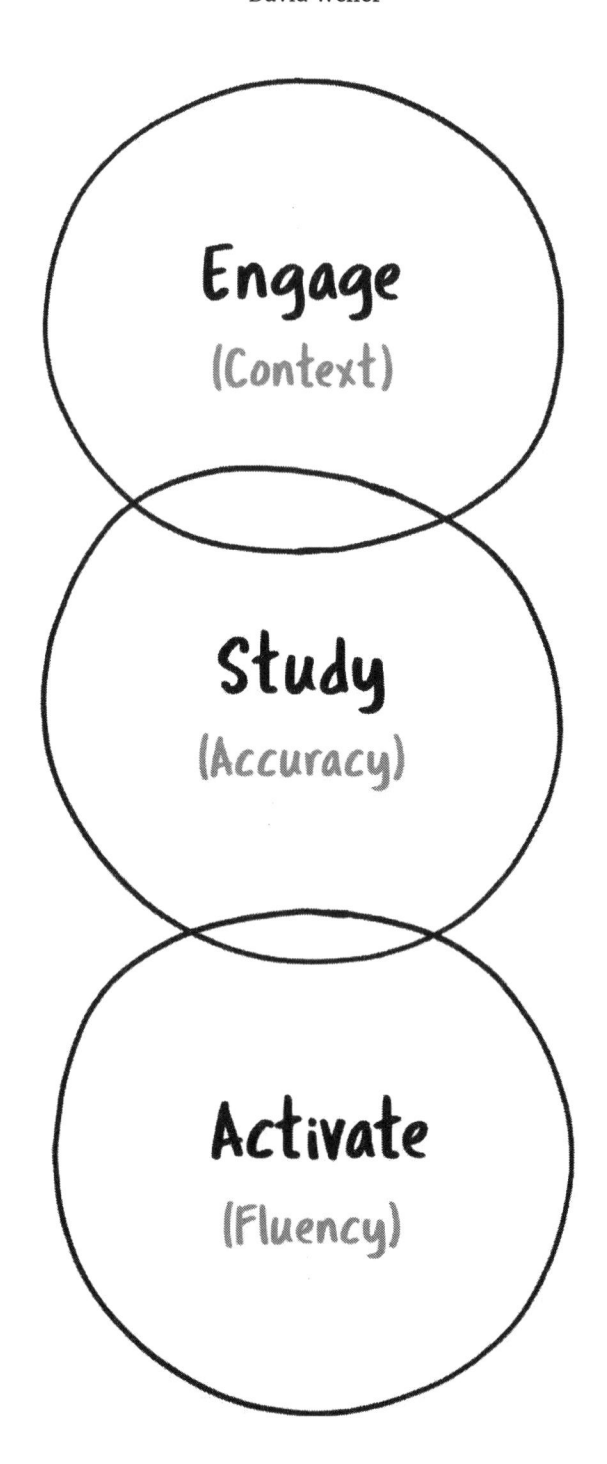

Study
(Accuracy)

Activate
(Fluency)

5.3
Engage, Study, Activate

At first glance, ESA appears to be the same as Presentation, Practice, Production.

While each stage roughly corresponds to PPP, ESA's stages are like Lego bricks, fitting together in multiple ways ((Harmer 2010: 54)

Let's look at each stage in turn, and then how they can fit together.

Stage 1: Engage

This is the stage where you get the learners interest; you 'engage' the students. If it's at the beginning of the lesson, it's also where you'll set the context.

You can engage learners using things like stories, anecdotes, music, discussion, photos or videos.

It's also about personalisation – encouraging learners to relate the material to themselves, or making predictions about the materials and lesson.

The focus of this stage is building engagement.

Stage 2. Study

This is the equivalent to both the 'Practice' and 'Production' stages of a PPP lesson. Learners should look at the target language, notice how it looks or sounds, and make sure they can produce it accurately.

The focus is on accuracy of the target language.

3. Activate

This is the equivalent of the 'Production' stage of a PPP lesson.

Students do activities that involve communication, and that everyone can participate in. They can use any language that they need to complete the activity.

Activities could be used are role-plays, creating dialogues or email exchanges, designing adverts or debates.

The focus of this stage is on communication and fluency.

Mixing it Up

I said the ESA structure is like Lego - you can assemble the stages in various orders, to make different sequences.

There are three common sequences: straight arrow, boomerang, and patchwork (Harmer 2010, 54).

Straight Arrow

This one is simple - the stages go in order, 'Engage' to 'Study' to 'Activate'.

An example for a low-level class to practice 'can / can't.

1. **Engage** - watch short video to set the context and engage.

2. **Study** - show a photo of a character from the video. Can and can't are used to describe her. Teacher makes sure the students can use correctly.
3. **Activate** – group work to design and describe a character, which they present to the class.

Boomerang

An example would be **E – A – S – A**.

Here the students would be engaged, then do a task, focus on form, and then do another task, with (hopefully) improved accuracy.

This is reminiscent of a Test-Teach-Test structure (which we'll see next).

Patchwork

An example would be **E – A – S – A – S – E**

This one looks like it's lost the plot, but it's about responding to learners and the tasks they're doing.

If you think that students will need some help with accuracy, put in a 'Study' stage. Getting bored? Put in an 'Engage' stage.

Overall, it's a flexible model that can be used with any kind of lesson.

Test
(Context, Observe)

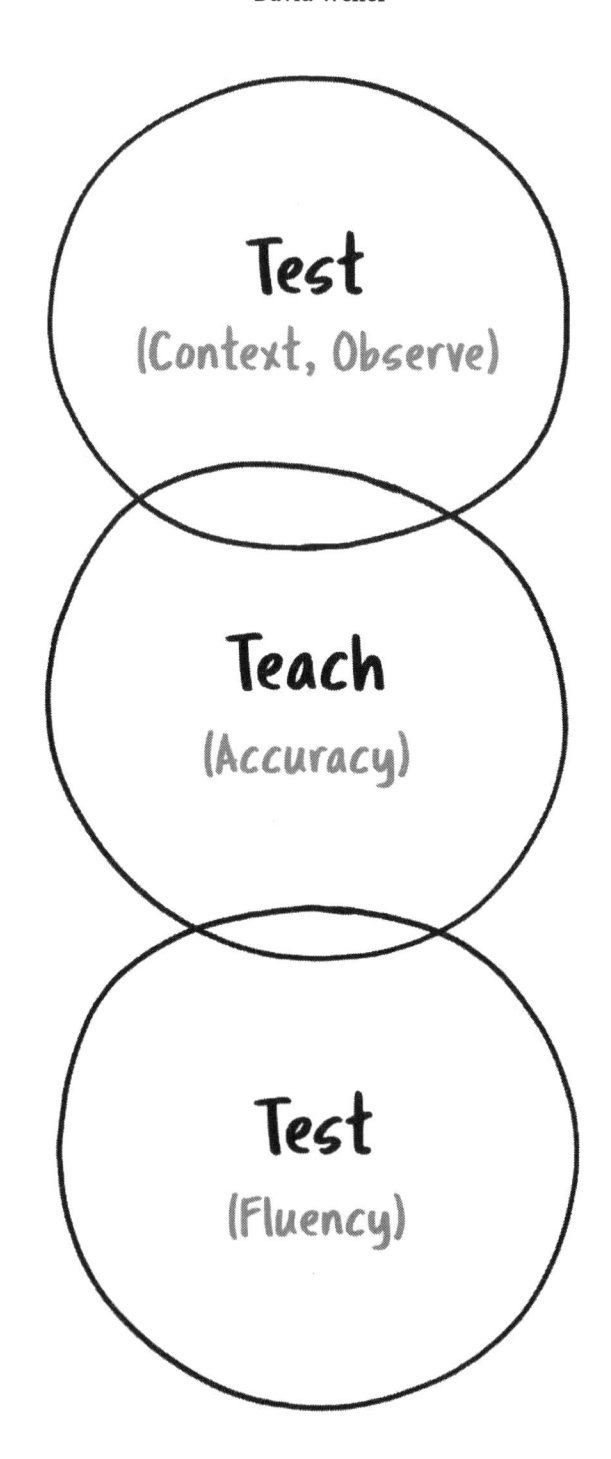

Teach
(Accuracy)

Test
(Fluency)

5.4
Test, Teach, Test

Students to use the language as best they can, then focus on accuracy, and then do a similar (or the same) task again with better results.

Stage 1: Test (1)

This first 'test' stage should introduce a context, and give the students a chance to do a task or activity.

'Test' doesn't have to be a test, it can be any activity with an information gap, opinion gap or knowledge gap (more about this in 'Task Design', p.73).

A bonus tip: if you select the topic and context carefully, it can steer the learners towards your intended target language. For example, a context where the learners must 'give advice' to each other would hopefully encourage the use of modal verbs ("You could / should / must" etc), which you'd then hear how well they could use in this activity

While this is a bonus, it's not always possible.

While students do the task, listen for errors in how they use the language, particularly the target language that you want to focus on. It's useful to jot these down, as you can use them in the next stage.

The aim for this stage is to observe errors that students make with the target language.

Stage 2: Teach

This stage is the equivalent of 'Presentation' from the 'Presentation, Practice, Production'.

You've got two options here. If the learners made errors with the language you thought they would, you can go ahead and 'teach' the target language to the learners in this stage.

Or, if they made errors that you feel are more important (i.e. they impede fluency even more than the language you anticipated teaching), focus on those instead.

Either option, this means a focus on form, and accuracy.

You could:

- Do delayed error correction with the examples of language from the last stage (elicit the errors, or peer correction)

- Explicitly tell the learners the target language, form, usage

- Give learners examples (on the board, on worksheets) and ask them to spot the patterns and work out the usage

- Drills, individual and choral

- Do gap-fills, cloze activities, or other worksheets

- Anything else that you'd normally do!

Don't forget to ask concept checking questions, and check that the weaker learners understand.

The focus for this section is accuracy.

Stage 3: Test (2)

Finally, the learners should do another task (or the same one as before) that encourages the use of the target language that they've just been focusing on.

Again, monitor the students and you should (hopefully!) see that their accuracy has improved.

The aim for this stage is fluency with improved accuracy.

Thoughts on Test, Teach, Test

TTT pairs nicely with classes that you don't know well, as the first stage allows you to observe them in action.

It's also great to use with unconfident learners, as they can see / hear their progress in one lesson. Especially if you use the same task for both 'test' stages, it's obvious to the students that they've improved.

I've also had good success with young learner classes that are a bit boisterous – the structure lends itself to good classroom management.

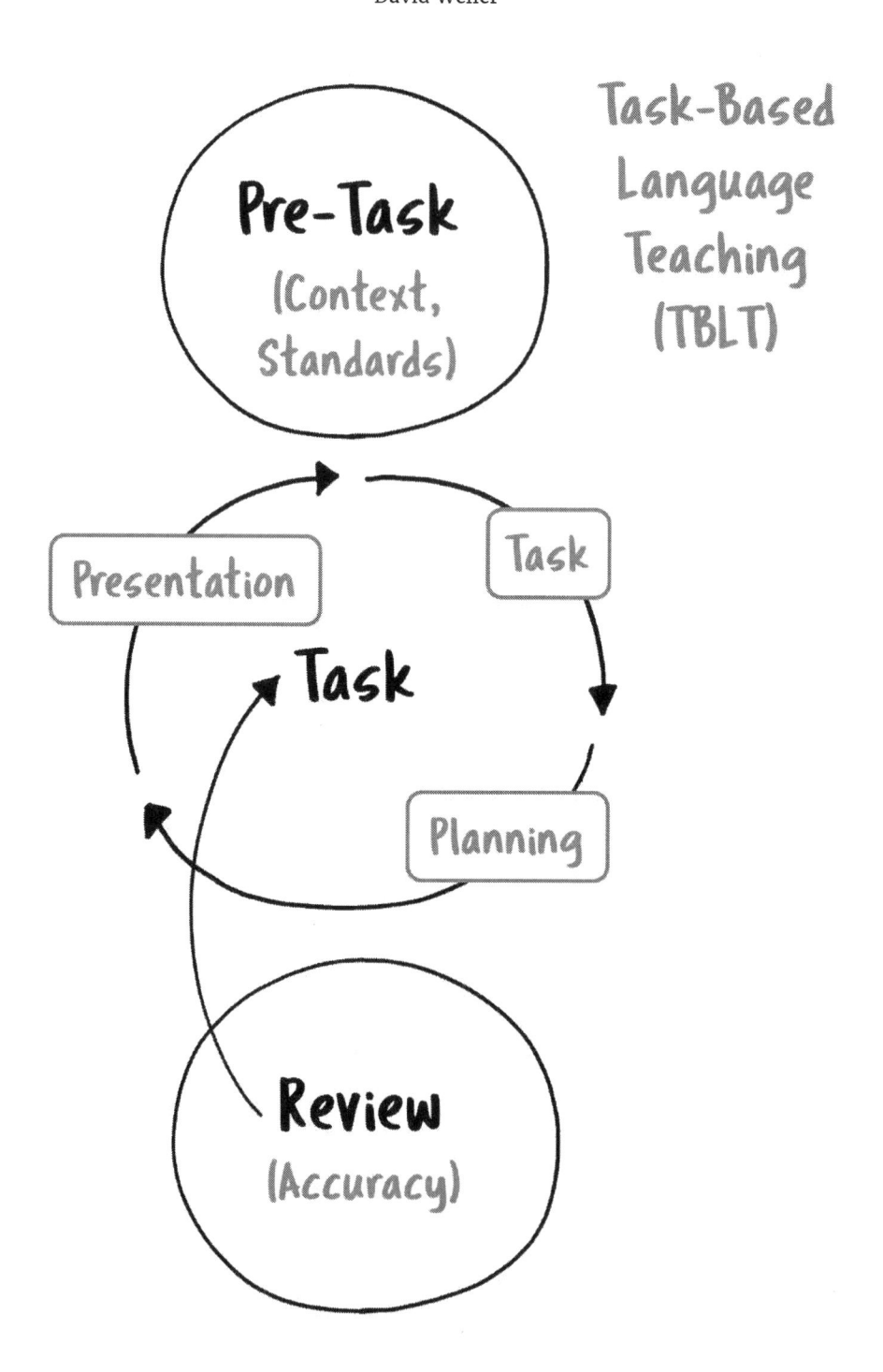

Task-Based Language Teaching (TBLT)

- **Pre-Task** (Context, Standards)
- Task
  - Presentation
  - Task
  - Planning
- **Review** (Accuracy)

5.5
Task Based Language Teaching

Task Based Language Teaching (TBLT) is an effective methodology, one that aligns with what we know about effective language learning (Long 2015: 8).

A TBLT lesson revolves around a meaningful task that requires students to use language to complete it. This is a more authentic use of language, in comparison with answering questions about grammar or vocabulary.

It's also a really nice way to get students engaged and using English more extensively. The collaborative element also builds confidence with language and social situations.

Let's jump straight in.

What is a Task?

Good question. TBLT calls for tasks that fit these requirements (Skehan 2004):

- It involves meaningful communication
- There's a 'gap' between students, to prompt communication. This 'gap' could be a difference of opinion, or knowledge
- Students can choose how to complete it, and which language they use to do so
- There's a clear goal, so students know when it's completed

Examples are creating a presentation, a piece of text, or a recorded dialogue.

Or trying to work out the solution to a practical problem, (like planning a complex journey), or deducing missing information (like working out who started a rumour).

It could even be justifying and supporting an opinion, like arguing for your preference in an election or favourite competitor in a TV show.

Like other methodologies, TBLT has three stages:

Stage 1. The Pre-Task

This is where you introduce a context and task to the students. Once they're engaged, set your expectations for the task. Setting expectations is important so the 'less motivated' students don't do the bare minimum.

To do this, you could show the students an example of the completed task, or model it.

If you want to differentiate your students (see p.96), then now is a good time to hand out support materials, or scaffold (see p.93) the task appropriately. Group them and give instructions.

The focus of the stage is to engage, set expectations and give instructions.

Stage 2. The Task

Begin the task!

Small groups or pairs are good, rather than a bigger group where shyer students can hide. Ideally you won't join in, but will be monitoring, and only giving hints if students get really stuck.

As part of the task, students will have to plan on how to complete it.

Once complete, the learners can present their accomplishment to others (optional).

A note here on task design – there are several ways to go about designing a task, but usually it should involve a 'gap' of some sort. See Task Design on p.73

The focus of this stage is fluency.

Stage 3. A Review

Once the learners have completed the task and have something to show, then it's time for a review.

Peer reviews are preferable, or if during your monitoring you see an error common to many, a teacher-led delayed correction is also very useful.

For weaker groups, peer correction can be made more effective by giving the students support on how to give feedback – perhaps via a checklist, or a 'Things to Look For' list.

The aim for this stage is accuracy, reflection and analysis.

Advantages of TBLT

- Student interaction is 'built in' to the lesson, as they need to communicate to complete the task
- Students' communication skills improve
- Students' confidence can improve, as tasks can mimic real life situations
- Students' motivation can improve due to the same reason
- Students' understanding of language becomes deeper, as it's used in realistic contexts

Disadvantages of TBLT

- Tasks must be carefully planned to meet the correct criteria
- It can take longer to plan overall
- It's time consuming adapting PPP-style course book lessons
- Too much scaffolding in the early stages can turn a TBL class into a PPP class
- Students can avoid using target language if they're not motivated (or too excited), or the tasks aren't well-designed

I've noticed three main ways that TBLT classes can be unsuccessful. Here they are, with potential solutions.

Reason 1. Tasks Aren't Well Designed

What happens: if tasks don't need students to cooperate to complete them, then students will often work by themselves.

Why it happens: there's no gap in the task (Task Design, p.73)

Solution: design your task with a communicative gap.

Reason 2. Students are 'Lazy' or Bored

What happens: Students do the bare minimum to complete the task. They use the simplest language they know, even single word utterances and body language, to get by.

Why it happens: the topic isn't interesting, hasn't been presented clearly, they don't understand, or there's no rapport with the teacher.

Solution: choose an interesting topic / context / material for learners, grade your language appropriately, check your instructions, and work on building rapport and engagement.

3. Students are too Excited

What happens: students are so excited to complete a task that they revert to a mixture of English, their first language and body language, shouting ("That.. Here! No, wrong, it, it - [speaks own language] - ta-da! Teacher, teacher, done!")

Why it happens: well, they're over-excited and just want to complete the task as soon as possible. The good news is that you chose a topic, context and materials that really connected with them - congratulations! Bad news is, it got out of hand.

Solution: If you expect that your task will make the students a little excited, make sure that you set the standards very clearly. Show a model of some kind, and be clear about the minimum standard. If appropriate, quantify it; "you have to record at least 20 lines of speech, everyone must speak at least three times..." and so on.

Thoughts on TBLT

- With advanced learners that are enthusiastic, a model isn't as important, and might even be a bad idea. Giving a model can steer your students in a particular direction, as they think that's what you want, and try to please you. Not giving a model lets them really use their imagination and creativity.

- Conversely, for younger or weaker learners, a model is necessary or there's a danger of ending up with low quality work.

- You might have heard of 'Project Based Learning' (PBL) – the only real difference between that and Task Based Learning is that PBL is usually run over periods longer than just one lesson, and with more review stages.

6. ACTIVITIES, EXERCISES, TASKS & MATERIALS

6.1
Definitions

Activities, exercises and tasks often defined in different ways.

Here, we'll use them in the following way:

Activity

An activity is anything that you want the learners to do that relates to them achieving the goals of the curriculum. It's a general term, and can include things like group discussions, games, debates, role-plays, etc.

Exercise

An exercise is something the students do that practices the language. It could be a drill, a listening or reading comprehension, or a gap-fill.

Task

A task is an activity that has a specific goal for the students. They should need to use their current language ability to complete it, and the focus should be on meaning.

6.2
Activities & Exercises

It's easy to get stuck using the same activities every lesson, but you don't need to condemn your students (and yourself!) to being bored.

Where can you find new ideas?

You can brainstorm ideas using an activities grid, like the one on the next page.

Across the top of the grid are the language skills. Down the side are the student interaction patterns (see p.85).

Each square needs an activity that practices that skill and student interaction pattern. For example, square 1 will involve the students practicing listening by themselves.

Now it's time to fill in the gaps!

Grab a few colleagues who complain that they never have enough activities. A workshop is ideal for this.

Ask pairs or small groups of teachers to brainstorm together and fill in the grids. There are only two rules:

	Individual	Pairs	Groups	Whole Class
Listening	1	2	3	4
Speaking	5	6	7	8
Reading	9	10	11	12
Writing	13	14	15	16
Grammar	17	18	19	20
Lexis	21	22	23	24
Pronunciation	**25**	**26**	**27**	**28**

- Every activity must be adaptable (i.e. it doesn't just work for a single grammar point or lexical set)

- Every activity must be fun, useful, or both.

Some activities will overlap, and that's fine. No need to be super strict, or quibble over categories. If an activity has both speaking and listening in equal amounts, you can put it in either.

Some examples, using the numbering from the grid, are on the next page.

A quick note: the difference between a whole class activity and individual is sometimes confusing. For a whole class activity, all students must be focused together (even if it's listening to one student). For an 'individual' activity every student is working by themselves at the same time.

#	Activity Overview
1	**Jigsaw Listening** Students piece together a story by listening to fragments they can play back from different stations around the room (or to audio sent to different groups' phones)
5	**Record & Compare** Students use their phones to record a sample of speech and compare it that spoken in a listening exercise. They notice what is / isn't different.
9	**Reading for Gist** Students have a limited time to scan a text for meaning. Each student has a text at their level (as authentic as possible) and thirty seconds to understand the context and content.

For more activities, you can visit the resources page for on my website: www.barefootteflteacher.com/bookresources

The password is: lessonplanning

6.3

More Activities

If sharing and brainstorming ideas with your colleagues doesn't work, then 'borrowing' might.

When even looking on the internet becomes too much like hard work, here are the best ways to liberate some activity ideas from your colleagues.

1. Start a discussion

In the staffroom, in the corridor or leaving work –ask a colleague what their current favourite activity is (and why!).

2. Brainstorm ideas in a workshop

Persuade your academic manager to have an 'activity sharing' workshop, where everyone must contribute their current favourite adaptable activity. Your manager will like it as it has zero preparation time for them, and it also falls under the remit of 'professional development'.

Teachers can demonstrate a five-minute activity, showing how they set up and run it using the other teachers as (un)willing participants.

Make sure someone takes notes and emails them around later - bonus points if you can get someone else to do it.

3. Look in shared computer folders.

If you use a shared computer drive, look in their files (or an old teachers' files who has left).

Underhanded perhaps, but effective nonetheless.

4. Impromptu peer observation

Ask one of your more relaxed colleagues if you can pop into their class when you're not teaching. Don't ask a new teacher though, they'll have a panic attack and jump out the nearest window.

Look for any activity that you haven't used, or one that's used in a different way. Jot down any unusual twists that you haven't seen before (keep an eye out for anything else useful too, like novel behaviour management techniques).

Oh, and don't fall asleep, it's impolite. Afterwards, a big thank you and an offer to return the favour goes a long way.

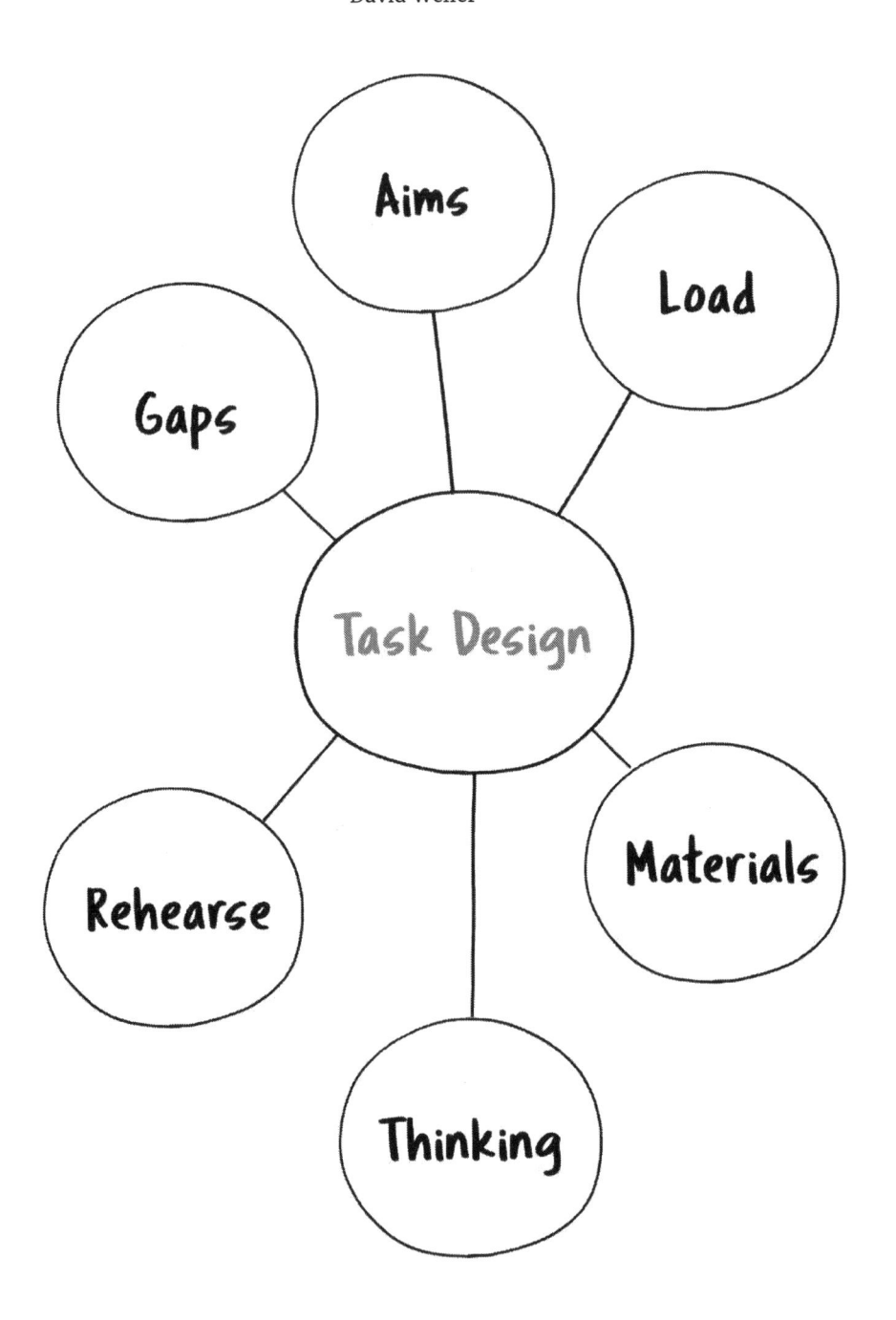

Task Design

- Aims
- Load
- Gaps
- Rehearse
- Materials
- Thinking

6.4
Task Design

One area of planning that often gets forgotten is task design. With everything else we need to focus on, it's usually an afterthought. Then we look for any activity that's loosely related to the lesson aim, and go with that.

Yet creating effective tasks is essential if you want students to learn.

Here are six principles that you can follow when designing tasks for your lessons.

1. Tasks Should Support Aims

Check - what will your task encourage students to think about? What language will it likely get them to produce?

- If it's too flashy, it might be so engaging that it distracts them and changes the subject
- If it's too boring, it won't engage them at all, and they'll get distracted
- Do the topic and context match the task?
- Are the students likely to produce the target language as they complete the task?

2. Tasks Need a Gap

Students need a reason to communicate. Sure, they'll talk if you tell them to ("discuss the topic with your partner!") but it won't be as engaging.

There are three types of gaps (Prabhu 1987):

- **Information Gaps**

Students have different information and must exchange that information to get a complete overview.

- **Reasoning Gaps**

Students must work out how to get from where they are, to where the task says they should be. An example would be planning a night out with restrictions on budget, timing, and other variables.

- **Opinion Gaps**

Students need to agree or disagree with others, and give reasons why. Debates, for example.

Any of these will provide a reason for students to communicate other than 'the teacher told me to speak, so I guess I'll have to'.

3. Plan for Students' Cognitive Load

As we mentioned when choosing aims, don't overwhelm students with too much information (a high cognitive load).

Sure, there's the intrinsic challenge of the tasks itself, known as intrinsic load (Sweller 1988) . That's fine, and it will encourage learning (see next point).

You can help students by removing 'extraneous cognitive load' from tasks – removing distractions, making sure instructions are clear, avoid dividing attention or having competing sources of information.

4. Consider What Students Will Think About

What are your students going to be thinking about while they're completing the task?

Cognitive psychology shows that what students think about, they remember (Willingham 2009). If tasks over-excite learners, or bore them, their thinking will veer away from the aims of the task.

If they're over-excited, they'll revert to using their first language to talk about the topic, or related topics.

If they're bored, they'll be thinking or talking about something else entirely.

5. Tasks Should Exploit Materials

Students need to understand the lesson, your instructions and the materials before even getting to the task.

So instead of then giving them new materials, could you re-use ones that you've already used in the lesson?

It'll reduce the amount of information, reducing the cognitive load on students.

As a bonus, you can keep it for the next time you have a similar lesson.

6. Mentally Rehearse Tasks

This sounds taxing, but it's quick, and helps to anticipate problems.

Close your eyes and imagine the class you're going to teach. Imagine all the personalities that make up the class. Now run through the task. Imagine:

- Introducing the task
- Giving instructions
- How the students will react
- The language they'll produce

From there, make any adjustments that you think will improve it.

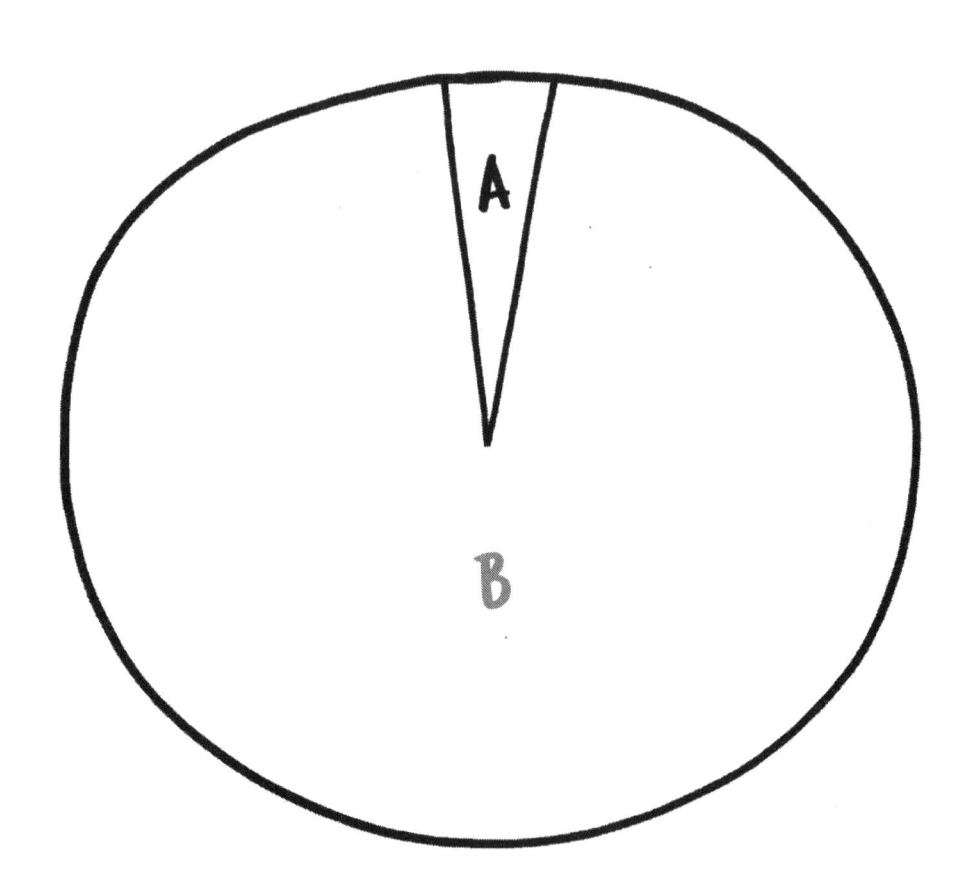

How I spend my planning time:

A: Lesson planning
B: Preparing materials

6.5
Using Materials

Using materials effectively is harder than it seems. From the teacher that staggers into class with a mountain of handouts, to the teacher that wanders in with nothing at all, I've seen (and done!) it all.

What I mostly see is teachers using materials reactively, rather than proactively.

What do I mean? I mean teachers who see an activity in the coursebook and think, 'Ah, I should really practice this. Quick, get a handout / worksheet / TV clip / whatever that has the same target language so learners can use it'.

They respond to the requirements of the course, rather than plan ahead.

And that's OK. But it could be so much better.

A proactive approach is looking at a lesson's aims, context, tasks, and then deciding on supplementary materials that can integrate into the whole lesson.

Instead of a band aid to prop up ailing attention, we can use materials to inspire learners to new heights – as well as doing a solid job of supporting the class aims, of course.

Materials Should Support Learning Aims by Being:

1. Engaging
2. A language model

3. Well designed (including cognitive load)

4. Exploitable

5. Differentiated

6. Authentic or Natural

Let's run through this list and talk about what each one really means.

1. Engaging

Materials have got to be interesting! Yes, I know it's easier to use the coursebook, but if it sends students to sleep, what's the point?

You need to know what your learners love to talk about.

You can use it as leverage to personalise materials and ramp up engagement, which increases their performance and gives you a much more enjoyable time as a teacher.

Unless your learners only like talking about the Kardashians. Then you're on your own.

2. A Language Model

It should go without saying that materials need accurate English. They serve as a model for your students, so mistakes in materials are ones you'll hear your students make.

3. Well-Designed

You don't need a degree in graphic design, but it helps if materials look good and elicit the desired response.

You should also consider the 'cognitive load' of the material. As we've said before in our aims and tasks, too much information can distract. Materials are a key part of this.

Can they be simplified? Can you remove unnecessary information? Materials with more than a couple of instructional sentences are liable to confuse instead of help. Can you let the structure, design, layout or graphics do the heavy lifting instead of explaining?

The gold standard of design is to have your learners intuitively 'get' what they need to do, so they can focus on the task rather than understanding the materials.

4. Exploitable

This is a critical concept to understand. The idea of using a material in your class multiple times, to illustrate different points, was a revelation to me when I first heard it. It expanded the way I thought about using materials in class.

The idea is that you're able to pull different aspects of language from the same material.

I still remember the first time I saw this happen. Students were asked to notice new vocabulary in a handout, which was clarified, then it was used to kickstart a discussion. Later, target grammatical structures were pulled from the same handout, and finally it was referred to as a model for a dialogue.

Talk about using materials effectively. My mind was blown.

Using material multiple times as a model for any 'final activity' you may have planned is incredibly helpful for weaker students in the class (B. Tomlinson 2011).

5. Differentiated or Scaffolded

A fancy term which means to account for different levels or abilities of student in your class. See page 93 for more on scaffolding and page 96 for differentiation.

You might have a handout with two versions, one of which offers more support for weaker learners. You need to pre-plan which version to give to which students, but this can pay dividends.

You'll have fewer 'fast-finishers' as stronger learners are stretched by the more challenging version.

6. Authentic or Natural

It's the eternal tug-o-war between authentic materials (that learners struggle with) vs inauthentic materials (that learners can understand).

The key is to be natural.

If you're recording a listening, don't sound like a robot. If you're writing a handout, don't use the target grammar structure so much that you sound like a crazy person. Try and keep it as natural as possible.

7. SUPPORTING STUDENTS

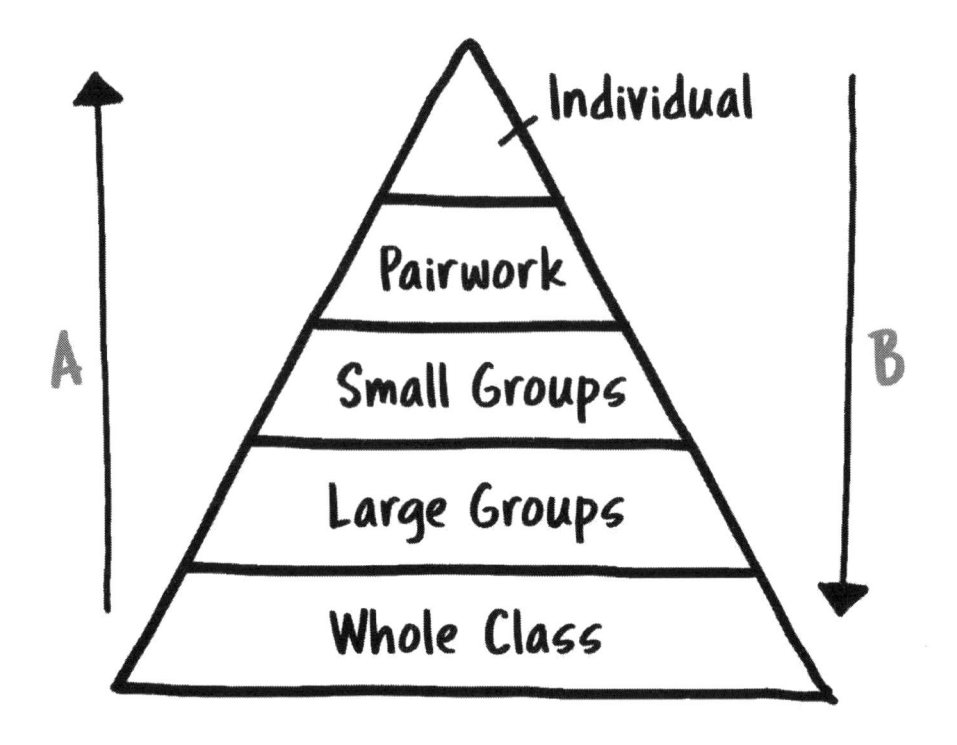

```
        Individual
       Pairwork
      Small Groups
      Large Groups
      Whole Class
```

A: Supportive - group practice before individual tasks.

B: Creative - individual practice before group tasks.

7.1
Interaction Patterns

Interaction patterns describe the number of students working together. Usually we talk about:

- Individual work (students work on their own)
- Pair work (two students work together)
- Small group work (3-5 students)
- Large group work (5+ students)
- Whole class (everyone together)

A rule of thumb is to have a mix of these patterns in a lesson. Too much of one interaction pattern and the lesson can be boring. Too many changes, and it can distract from the content.

One method is to put interaction patterns in a sequence, which can either support students, or encourage them to be creative.

The diagram on the previous page shows two sequences. 'A' starts with the whole class and then reduces the size of the groups as the task or lesson progresses. This lets students support each other for challenging activities. Larger groups mean students don't lose face, and they can cooperate to succeed.

'B' is the reverse, and encourages students to think for themselves before sharing and discussing with others.

Decide which sequence is best for the tasks that you want to do in the lesson.

Example: 'Supporting' with Interaction Patterns

When focusing on form, you might want to elicit from the whole class first, rather than pick on individuals (and putting them under a lot of pressure with a possibility of losing face if they get the answer wrong).

Then you might work to notice differences in two example sentences in a small group. That might be followed by working in pairs to produce a new, correct sentence. Finally, learners would do an individual exercise to practice.

A. Reasons to start with a whole class activity:

For a challenging activity that students might struggle with if you gave it to them as an individual activity immediately.

The sequence gives them a chance to practice in a 'safe' group setting first, then ups the involvement during small group / pair work, which should give them the confidence of doing the activity by themselves.

B. Reasons to start with individual work:

To be creative and prepare for a larger group or whole class activity.

Students can be creative and give their own input, have it multiplied by working in pairs or small groups, and then take part in a whole class activity, for example a debate, or any complex task-based activity.

Don't feel that you must use every stage of the sequence – some classes need less support or preparation time than others.

Boring

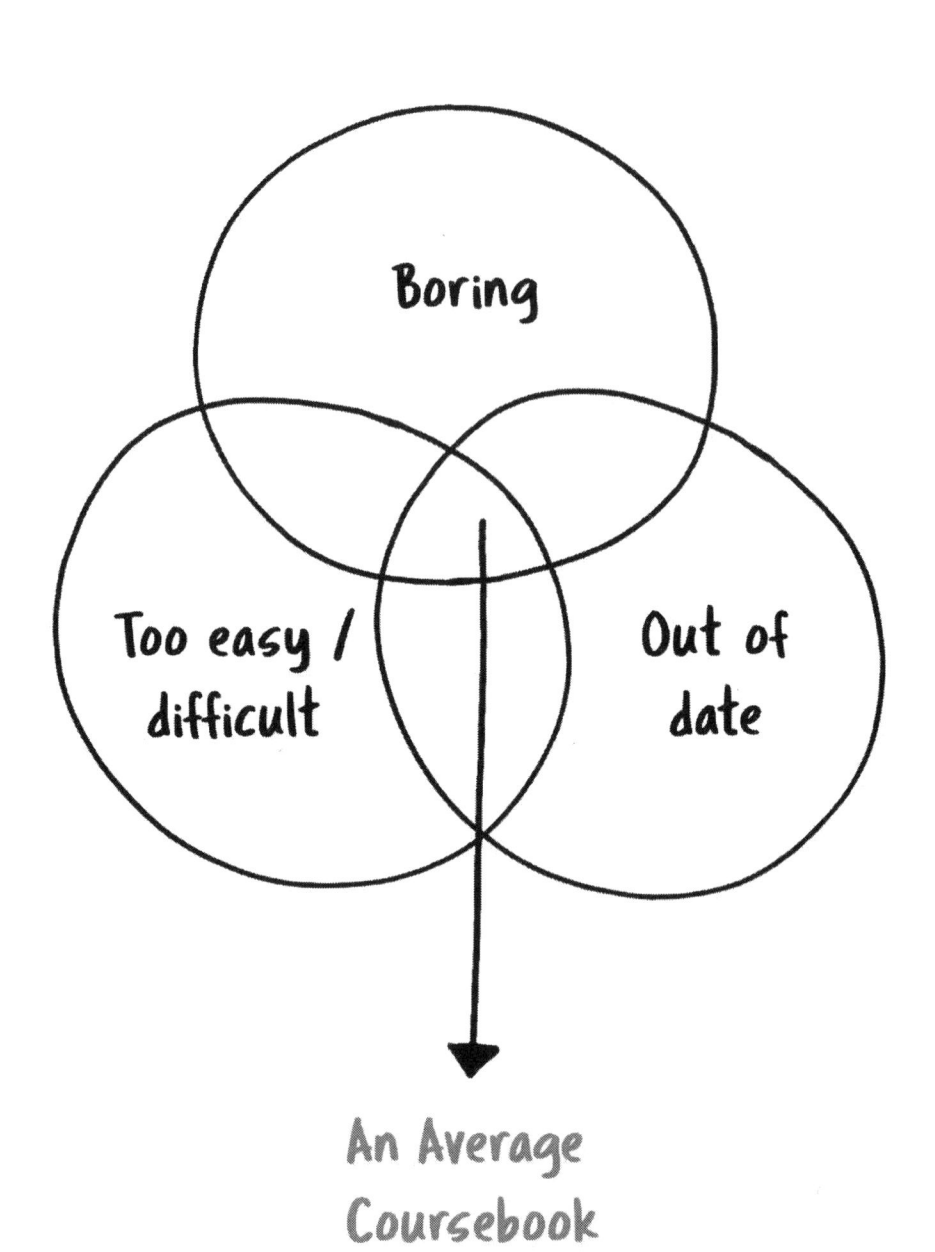

Too easy / difficult

Out of date

An Average Coursebook

7.2
Personalising the Coursebook

A lot of schools have a policy about how much of the coursebook you need to cover. A lot of teachers really don't like their coursebook.

So, the question is, how flexible are you allowed to be?

Whatever your answer, you should adapt the content as much as you feel is needed to make it relevant and engaging.

You can do this by 'personalising' or 'performing' the coursebook.

Personalising Coursebooks

Remember the 'four levels of language' we saw earlier? A lot of the time coursebooks don't give you one of those levels (i.e. a topic, context, function, or form) for every class. That's a good opportunity to choose the missing one with your students in mind.

You can also show your students how the topic relates to them. Find an interesting connection.

Another way is to bring the book up to date. If events, celebrities, TV shows, or technology used are out of date - modify them.

'Performing' the Coursebook

If you can't change the material you have to work with, at least you can make it more interesting.

Performing the coursebook works because you inject some life into what looks like boring material.

Some suggestions to liven up dull material:

- Perform a dramatic reading of a text.

- Ask students to act out a dialogue or text.

- 'Spot the difference' the coursebook text and another you've prepared

- Before you read a text, act it out and get the students to guess what you're miming

- Get students to update a boring text with cooler characters and local places

- Read aloud with voices of different (and funny) characters.

- Students perform a prequel or sequel to the text or dialogue

This list is to get you started – use your imagination to create more!

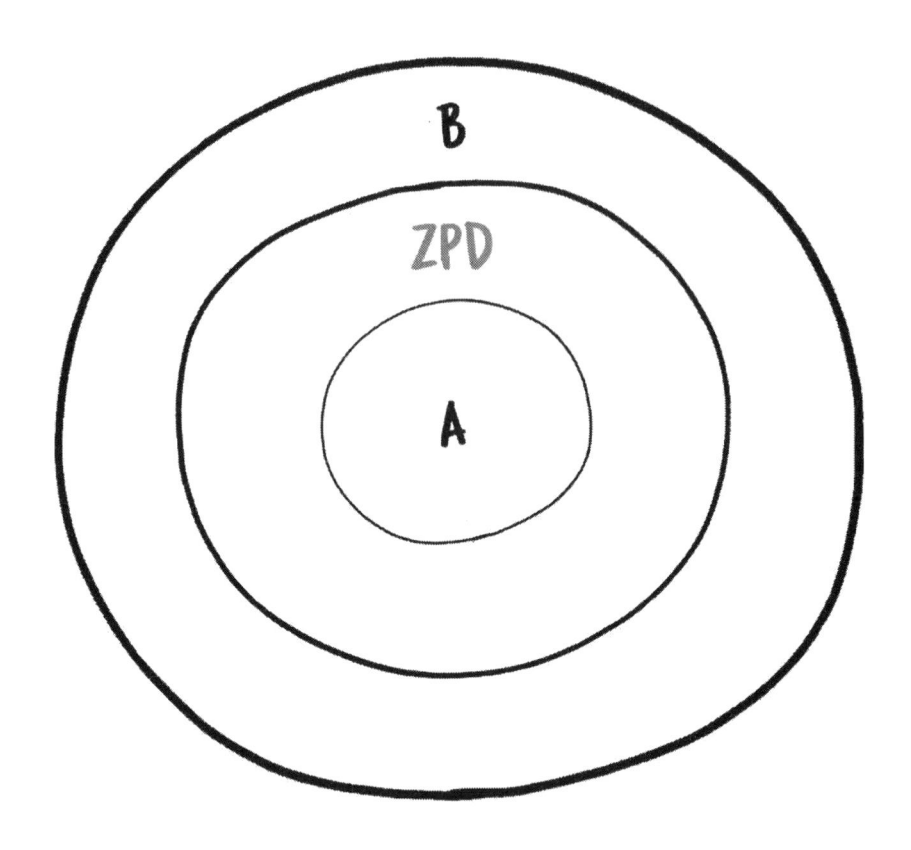

A: Stuff learners can do.
ZPD (Zone of Proximal Development): Stuff learners can do, with support.
B: Stuff learners can't do (even with support).

7.3
Scaffolding

'Scaffolding' is support that we give learners by breaking down a task into manageable chunks (Bransford, et al. 2000).

The term itself is a metaphor for support - just as scaffolding is put around a building that's being constructed, we provide support to learners while they work on understanding and using language.

By providing support, then gradually handing over more and more of the task to them, students will move from dependency to independence.

> "What a child can do today with assistance, she will be able to do by herself tomorrow."
> - Lev Vygotsky (Vygotskij and Cole 1981)

The idea of scaffolding came from the work of Lev Vygotsky, a psychologist in the early 20th century. He proposed a concept called the 'Zone of Proximal Development' (Berk and Winsler 1995).

Despite the complicated name, it explains a simple concept - that with help, students learn better with help from someone more knowledgeable, more than if they studied by themselves.

Examples of Scaffolding

A lot of activities that most of us do in a 'controlled practice' stage of the lesson would probably count as scaffolding. Controlled practice stages typically ask learners to practice a limited set of the target language, or to practice with the support of reference material. Then as we move to a freer practice in the latter half of the lesson, the controls on which language to use are dropped, or learners are asked not to refer to support material.

Some examples of TEFL scaffolding are:

- Give language prompts, or substitution drilling
- Let students use dictionaries or mobile phones to check language
- Allow students to check answers with a partner
- Activate students' prior knowledge and language related to the target topic
- Allow students a chance to plan an activity together
- Give specific models of language to use or work towards
- Pre-learning or the 'flipped classroom' approach for new lexis or grammar

Does Scaffolding Have any Disadvantages?

Only if it's misused. One way that this can happen is if the lesson and tasks are 'over supported', i.e. if too much help is given. If that happens, then you'll most likely see learners get bored and start to rely on the support, rather than think for themselves.

How do you know if it's too much? If your learners can't answer a question without referring to support material at the end of the class, it's too much.

Top Tips for Scaffolding

- Know your students' level
- Monitor closely (you can keep an eye on the level of challenge)
- Don't offer too much help, or students will come to rely on you.

7.4

Differentiation

Differentiation means teaching one concept and meeting the different learning needs in a group.

Your students may be different ages, genders, with different geographic and cultural backgrounds. They probably have differing abilities, their own hobbies, interests and passions.

So why would teaching them all the same way be logical?

How to Differentiate (1)

Established theory gives an outline of how to differentiate (C. A. Tomlinson 2014). First, you need to know your students. Specifically:

- **Readiness** - (how they perform, ability, pace of learning, independence level, etc.)
- **Interests**
- **Learning Profile** – which learning preferences do they have?

Then, based on your knowledge, you're able to differentiate students':

- **Content** – what they need to know, based on a curriculum
- **Process** – tiered activities based on 'readiness'

- **Product** – how they demonstrate what they've learned (i.e. the tasks)

- **Learning Environment** – seating, flexible groupings, atmosphere, etc.

How to Differentiate (2)

From my experience, I've found six ways to differentiate effectively, that look at differentiation from a different angle:

1. Time

Have an extension task ready for learners that finish first.

2. Task

Set groups different tasks, based on their linguistic ability. I normally have two or three groups (e.g. low, medium, high level groups).

3. Topic/Context

This is more differentiation by interest, or demographic.

Let's say we want to students to practice the function of making a complaint. If half the class are businesspeople, and half are university students, then create a different scenario for each group.

4. Material

Edit your materials so that they provide more (or less) support as needed.

Think of your worksheets, handouts, PPTs, even your listening and reading source material – all can be differentiated.

A worksheet can have a word bank with definitions in the students' language. You set your room up so you can play two different versions of a listening (or send it straight to students' phones). Use your imagination!

5. Groupings

Are you going to put students of a similar level together, or match stronger and weaker students together?

Both have their advantages and disadvantages, so be sure to vary.

6. Role

Allocate a stronger learner to each group of students, and give them a different role.

Perhaps as group leader, error-checker, or something where they have extra responsibility or different duties.

Thoughts on Differentiation

Yes, differentiation does take longer to plan than not differentiating.

Yes, it is a more delicate skill which is tough for newer teachers who are still mastering classroom management skills.

It is, however, a great tool to help support weaker students and push stronger learners even further.

Instead of 'teaching to the middle' as we often do, we don't let students fall behind, and we don't have to hold others back.

Which is a win-win, if you ask me.

Are Scaffolding and Differentiation Different?

Yes.

The goal for both is to provide customised support, so it's easy to see why these concepts can get confused.

Scaffolding involves breaking up a task, skill or language point into parts, and then give support to learners to master each part, and then the whole.

Differentiation techniques are wider ranging, as we've seen, and cater for different tasks, interests and roles as well.

Do they both work? Definitely (Hattie 2012).

Oh, and lastly, please don't differentiate by learning style. There's overwhelming evidence now that it's a 'neuromyth' – an outdated belief in education with no theoretical validity (Riener and Willingham 2010).

8. ASSESSMENT

8.1
Checking Understanding

If any of your students might not understand a new concept, check they understand before you move on.

'Do you understand?' doesn't cut it. Students will say yes, for an easy life.

You need proof that they understand, and the best way to get it is if they answer a question correctly. 'Concept Checking Questions' (or CCQs for short) are designed for this.

Rather than try and think of CCQs on the spot, it's easier to prepare them when you're planning.

Here are some guidelines:

- Be specific – does the question check what you want it to check?

- Don't use the target language to ask about the target language.

- Use simpler language that you know learners will understand

- They should be answerable with one or two words

- They should be short

You can create CCQs by breaking down the item you want to check into its concepts, then turning those concepts into questions.

For example, the word 'motorbike'. A motorbike has two wheels, can go as fast as a car, and isn't a bicycle. So, after you've introduced the concept, you could ask:

- How many wheels does it have?
- Can it go as fast as a car?
- Is it the same as a bicycle?

Don't be like the teacher trying to concept check 'cat'. The teacher asked, "what's the opposite of a dog?" to which the student answered... "Um... no dog?"

Smart student, but not the answer the teacher was hoping for. Be sure to think through your CCQs.

8.2
Checking Progress

How will you know your students are learning?

If your plan goes perfectly, it's still possible that they don't learn a thing.

Student activity, engagement and confidence – these don't guarantee students are learning (Fletcher-Wood 2018).

When you're planning, think about what evidence you'll need to see or hear to be certain learning is taking place. Here are some ways you can do just that.

Monitoring

During exercises and tasks, walk around the classroom. Get close enough so you can hear or see, not so close that students stop and give you funny looks.

Look and listen what language the students are producing. You'll be able to tell whether they're on track, doing better or worse than you were expecting. You'll also be able to notice any errors or mistakes that they're making.

Combine this with error correction and you have a winning formula.

Peer Assessment

If you include peer assessment in your activities, congratulations! You're officially awesome.

Peer assessment is a powerful tool for students to develop their language accurately. In an exercise where you've set the target language and standards, you can ask students to correct each other when they make a slip with the target language.

At first students might be hesitant to correct each other, but if you demonstrate by asking a student to correct you (and then make some silly mistakes), they'll soon come around. Especially if it becomes a regular part of your lessons.

Some more tips:

- Be sure that students know the correct form
- Don't ask them to correct more than one thing at once
- Ask them to correct in a manner that they would like to be corrected
- Pair students of a similar level together

Again, monitor to make sure they're doing it correctly.

End of Class Review

A quick five-minute review at the end of class can tell you if your lesson has been a success.

However you decide to review, remember that you want evidence of them using the target language.

Some review formats I've found successful:

3-2-1

Ask students to tell a partner (or write) three things they thought were interesting, two things they learnt and one question they have about anything from the class.

Like / Dislike / Learn

A similar format, where students say one thing they liked, one they didn't (great for getting feedback on your teaching!) and one thing they learnt.

Another Context

Students work in pairs and have two minutes to use the target language in a different context.

Exit Ticket

With this strategy, students must answer a question before they can leave the classroom.

This can be formal, where students have a slip of paper to write on that they give you. I prefer an informal approach, where you ask the students out loud. This way you can differentiate the questions, making them as challenging as necessary. The spoken approach is great for young learners, and you can give them a high five on the way out.

What you think will happen (your lesson plan)

What actually happens (your lesson)

8.3
Self-Assessment

Class is over, you've high-fived your students and bounced into the staffroom. What next?

Tempting as it is to grab a coffee and start prepping for the next class, take a minute and scribble some notes on your lesson plan.

What went well? What didn't? Why? What could be improved?

What do you want to remember when you teach this lesson next time? (how did the context work? Would the lesson work better with a different structure? Etc.)

What do you want to know when you teach this group of students again? (Did you learn anything new about their motivations? Should you never, ever sit Sally next to Simon again? Etc)

Think in terms of everything you've learned about planning, and what will help you deliver a better lesson the next time around.

9. REVIEW

9.1
What If I'm Too Busy to Plan?

I get it. I've been there, many times. The working conditions a lot of us face mean planning time is sometimes short, or non-existent.

Teacher shortages. Intensive summer or winter sessions. Sick colleagues.

Many times, I've been told something like, "Jeff's called in sick. You're teaching in two minutes in classroom 5. Level 2A."

What do you do? In an emergency like this, there's nothing else you can do but plan as you walk to the classroom.

Ask yourself the four fundamental questions:

1. What do you know about the students?
2. Where do you want them to get to by the end of the lesson?
3. What's the best way for them to get there?
4. How can you check their progress?

Of course, this isn't ideal, but reality does throw us into situations like this. Having a planning process can make the difference between chaos and some semblance of a decent lesson.

The basic planning process in this book can be scaled from zero planning time to full and detailed lesson plans for when you're being observed.

At the other end, if you have a planned observation coming up and want to make sure you haven't missed anything, use the checklist in the next chapter. It'll also help you justify your planning process, if asked.

9.2
Lesson Planning Checklist

Students

- What do you know about your students?
    - Their background?
    - Level of English?
    - Motivation?

Aims

- What will students be better able to do by the end of the lesson?
- Is it required by the syllabus / curriculum?
- Is it student centred?
- Is it specific?
- Is it observable?
- What's the topic?
- What's the context?
- What's the function?
- What's the form? Grammar, phonology or lexis?
    - Grammar
    - Phonology
    - Vocabulary / Lexis?
- What do you want to improve at in this lesson?

Context
- How does the context relate to the learners?
- Is it a strong context?
- Is it real, realistic, implied or imaginary?
- How will you set the context – verbally, visually, aurally or using realis?
- How are you going to run the context through the lesson?

Structure
- Which lesson structure are you going to adapt?
- Why?
- Can you put your exercises and tasks (below) into this structure?

Exercises
- Which exercises will help them practice this language (can you break it down to help them?)

Tasks
- Which task (or tasks) will get students to demonstrate that they've reached the lesson aims?

Materials
- Do your materials engage and support students?
- Can you re-use material?

Supporting Students
- Have you varied interaction patterns to support students, or encourage creativity?
- Have you personalised the coursebook?
- Have you scaffolded where needed?
- Do you need to differentiate any parts of the lesson?

Assessment
- How are you going to check students understand new language?
- How are you going to check students have made progress?
- How are you going to review at the end of the lesson?

9.3
Final Thoughts

I hope you've found some ideas from reading this.

Lesson planning seems simple, but has layers of complexity that take a long time to master. The key to improving is to keep putting into action ideas you get. Learn what works for you and your teaching style.

If you'd like to read more about any of the topics here, the bibliography is a good place to start.

If you've found this book useful, please consider leaving me a short review on Amazon.

Good luck, and good planning.

9.4
Resources

Email Me
What did you think? Let me know at davidweller@pm.me
I read every email, and I'll do my best to respond.

Book Resources
You can find resources from the book at:
www.barefootTEFLteacher.com/bookresources
The password is: lessonplanning

Find Me on Twitter
I go by @BarefootTEFL. I tweet language teaching and learning news and articles I come across.

Browse my Blog
I write regularly at www.barefootTEFLteacher.com

Sign Up to My Newsletter
You can find a sign-up box on the blog sidebar. I send a newsletter a month, where I share news and updates from the world of language teaching.

REFERENCES

Ausubel, David. 1968. *Educational Psychology. A Cognitive View.* New York: Holt, Rinehart and Winston, Inc.

Berk, Laura E., and Adam Winsler. 1995. *Scaffolding Children's Learning: Vygotsky and Early Childhood Education.* NAEYC Research into Practice Series, v. 7. Washington: National Association for the Education of Young Children.

Bransford, John, National Research Council (U.S.), and National Research Council (U.S.), eds. 2000. *How People Learn: Brain, Mind, Experience, and School.* Expanded ed. Washington, D.C: National Academy Press.

Cook, Vivian. 2013. *Second Language Learning and Language Teaching.* 4. ed. London: Routledge.

Fletcher-Wood, Harry. 2018. *Responsive Teaching: Cognitive Science and Formative Assessment in Practice.* Abingdon, Oxon ; New York, NY: Routledge.

Harmer, Jeremy. 2010. *How to Teach English.* New ed., 6. impr. How to ... Series. Harlow: Pearson Longman.

Hattie, John. 2012. *Visible Learning for Teachers: Maximizing Impact on Learning.* London ; New York: Routledge.

Long, Michael H. 2015. *Second Language Acquisition and Task-Based Language Teaching*. First Edition. Chichester, West Sussex [England] ; Malden, MA: Wiley-Blackwell.

Odell, Lee, John E Warriner, and Rinehart Holt and Winston, Inc. 2007. *Elements of Language. First Course First Course*. Orlando, Fla.: Holt, Rinehart and Winston.

O'Neill, Jan. 2000. 'SMART Goals, SMART Schools'. *Educational Leadership* 57 (5): 46–50.

Prabhu, N. S. 1987. *Second Language Pedagogy*. Oxford ; New York: Oxford University Press.

Richards, Jack C., and Willy A. Renandya, eds. 2013. *Methodology in Language Teaching: An Anthology of Current Practice*. 1st publ., 17. print. Cambridge: Cambridge Univ. Press.

Riener, Cedar, and Daniel Willingham. 2010. 'The Myth of Learning Styles'. *Change: The Magazine of Higher Learning* 42 (5): 32–35. https://doi.org/10.1080/00091383.2010.503139.

Skehan, Peter. 2004. *A Cognitive Approach to Language Learning*. Oxford Applied Linguistics. Oxford: Oxford Univ. Press.

Sweller, John. 1988. 'Cognitive Load during Problem Solving: Effects on Learning'. *Cognitive Science* 12 (2): 257–85. https://doi.org/10.1016/0364-0213(88)90023-7.

Tomlinson, Brian, ed. 2011. *Materials Development in Language Teaching*. 2nd ed. Cambridge Language Teaching Library. Cambridge, N.Y: Cambridge University Press.

Tomlinson, Carol A. 2014. *The Differentiated Classroom: Responding to the Needs of All Learners*. 2nd edition. Alexandria, VA: ASCD.

Vygotskij, Lev Semenovič, and Michael Cole. 1981. *Mind in Society: The Development of Higher Psychological Processes*. Nachdr. Cambridge, Mass.: Harvard Univ. Press.

Willingham, Daniel T. 2009. *Why Don't Students like School? A Cognitive Scientist Answers Questions about How the Mind Works and What It Means for the Classroom*. 1st ed. San Francisco, CA: Jossey-Bass.

ABOUT THE AUTHOR

David Weller started teaching in 2003 and has since been a language teacher, trainer, manager, materials developer, examiner, moderator, speaker and blogger.

Along the way he gained a Trinity Diploma in TESOL and a Masters in TESOL.

Originally from the UK, he's fascinated by the mystery of learning, language, culture, and helping others develop.

David Weller

Printed by Amazon Italia Logistica S.r.l.
Torrazza Piemonte (TO), Italy